Lonely Planet

≋ *Fast Talk*

Norwegian

Guaranteed to get you talking

Contents

⇒ Special Features

Before You Go

Many visitors to Norway get around without speaking a word of Norwegian, but just a few phrases go a long way in making friends, inviting service with a smile, and ensuring a rich and rewarding travel experience.

Norway has two official written language forms. They are very similar, and every Norwegian learns both at school. Bokmål (BM), literally 'book-language', is the urban-Norwegian variety of Danish, the language of the former rulers of Norway. It's the written language of 80 percent of the population. Although many Norwegians speak a local dialect in the private sphere, most of them speak BM in the public sphere. BM is therefore very appropriate for the traveller who wants to communicate with Norwegians all over the country.

The other written language is Nynorsk (NN), or 'New Norwegian' – as opposed to Old Norwegian, the language in Norway before 1500 AD, that is, before Danish rule. It's an important part of Norwegian cultural heritage as it is the truly 'Norwegian' language, as opposed to the Danish-based BM.

In speech the distinction between BM and NN is no problem since Norwegians understand either. Many people are put off trying to speak Norwegian because of the two languages, but in reality, BM is the ruling language. This book uses BM only.

In the rural areas you may come across people who hardly speak a word of English, and if you show an effort to speak Norwegian, it will help a great deal to establish contact. Many Norwegians will answer you in English, as they are only too eager to show off their knowledge. Their use of English is usually very good.

If you read our coloured pronunciation guides as if they were English, you'll be understood.

PRONUNCIATION TIPS

★ Nearly all vowels in Norwegian have short and long versions. This can affect the meaning, so look at the word carefully.

★ Length, as a distinctive feature of vowels, is very important in the pronunciation of Norwegian. Almost every vowel has a (very) long and a (very) short counterpart, when appearing in a stressed syllable. Generally, it's long when followed by one consonant, and short when followed by two or more consonants.

Fast Talk Norwegian

Don't worry if you've never learnt Norwegian before – it's all about confidence. You don't need to memorise endless grammatical details or long lists of vocabulary – you just need to start speaking. You have nothing to lose and everything to gain when the locals hear you making an effort. And remember that body language and a sense of humour have a role to play in every culture.

"you just need to start speaking"

Even if you use the very basics, such as greetings and civilities, your travel experience will be the better for it. Once you start, you'll be amazed how many prompts you'll get to help you build on those first words. You'll hear people speaking, pick up sounds and expressions from the locals, catch a word or two that you know from TV already, see something on a billboard – all these things help to build your understanding.

5. Phrases to Learn Before You Go

1. How do you say ... ?
Hvordan sier du?

voorr-dahn *see*-ehrr doo?

Making an effort to speak the language is always appreciated and Norwegians are usually happy to help.

2. What would you recommend?
Hva anbefaler du?

vah *ahn*-beh-fah-lehrr doo?

When in doubt, ask a local for advice.

3. One coffee (with milk), please
En kaffe (med melk), takk.

ehn kah-feh (may mehlk), tahk

If Norway has a national drink, it's coffee. Most Norwegians drink it black and strong, but foreigners requiring milk and sugar are normally indulged.

4. Where are the toilets?
Hvor er toalettene?

voorr aar too-ah-*leh*-teh-neh?

This phrase is an oldie but a goodie.

5. Shall I take my shoes off?
Skal jeg ta av skoene mine?

Skahl yai ta ahv *skoo*-eh-neh *mee*-neh?

Norwegians usually take their shoes off when entering someone's home, particularly when the weather is wintry.

6

10. Phrases to Sound Like a Local

Hey! **Hei!** hai

Great! **Supert!** soo-parrt

Sure. **Ok** oo-koh/oh-kai

No way! **Er det sant?** ehrr day sahnt

Just joking! **Bare tuller.** bah-rreh tü-lehrr

No problem. **Ingen problem.** ing-ehn proo-blehm

Well done! **Bra jobba!** brrah jo-bah

What a shame. **Det var synd.** day vahrr sün

Not bad. **Ikke så verst.** i-keh soh varsht

Maybe. **Kanskje** kahn-sheh

10. Phrases to Start a Sentence

When is (the tour)?	Når er (omvisningen)? norr arr (*ohm*-vees-ning-ehn)?
Where is (the bus stop)?	Hvor er (bussholdeplassen)? voorr arr (*bus*-hoh-leh-plahs-ehn)?
Where can I (put this)?	Hvor kan jeg (legge dette)? voorr kahn yai (*leh*-geh *deh*-teh)?
Do you have (a map)?	Har du (et kart)? hahrr du (eht kahrt)?
Is there (a bus to...)?	Er det (en buss til...)? arr day (ehn bus til)?
I'd like (a one-way ticket)	Jeg vil gjerne ha (en enveisbillett) yai vil *yarr*-neh hah (ehn *ehn*-vais-bi-*leh*)
I'd like to (pay the bill).	Jeg vil gjerne (betale regningen). yai vil *yarr*-neh (beh-*tah*-leh *rrai*-ning-ehr
Can I (take this)?	Kan jeg (ta dette)? kahn yai (*tah* deh-teh)?
Do I need to (book)?	Må jeg (bestille)? moh yai (beh-*sti*-leh)?
Can you (show me)?	Kan du (vise meg)? kahn du (*vee*-seh mai)?

Chatting & Basics

≡ Fast Phrases

Hello.	Goddag.
	goo-*dahg*.
Goodbye.	Ha det.
	hah-day.
Do you speak English?	Snakker du engelsk?
	snah-kehrr du *ehng*-ehlsk?

Essentials

Yes.	Ja.
	yah.
No.	Nei.
	nai.
Please.	Vær så snill.
	varr shoo *snil*.
Thank you.	Takk.
	tahk.
You're welcome.	Vær så god.
	varr-shoo-*goo*.
Excuse me.	Unnskyld.
	un-shül.
Sorry. (forgive me)	Beklager.
	beh-*klah*-gehrr.

Fast Talk — Pronunciation

Below is a general pronunciation guide of Norwegian sounds, used in the simplified transliterations throughout the book. Consonants not listed here are pronounced as in English.

Vowels

ah	as the 'a' in 'father'
uh	as the 'u' in 'cut'
a	as the 'a' in 'act'
eh	as the 'e' in 'bet'
ee	as the 'ee' in 'seethe'
i	as the 'i' in 'hit'
ü	a bit like the 'e' in British English 'dew' – try pursing your lips and saying 'ee'
o	a short 'o' as in 'pot'
oh	as the 'o' in 'note'
oo	a long 'oo' as in 'cool'
u	a short 'oo' as in 'foot'
ö	as the 'e' in 'summer'
or	as the 'or' in 'for', with less emphasis on the 'r'
er	as the 'er' in 'fern' but shorter, without the 'r'

Diphthongs

ae	as the 'ea' in 'bear'
ay	as the 'ay' in 'day'
ai	as the sound of 'eye'
oy	the 'oy' as in 'toy'
ow	as the 'ou' in 'out'

Semiconsonants

w	as in 'wet'
y	as in 'yet'

Consonants	
g	always a hard 'g' as in 'get', never as in 'gentle'
s	always as in 'kiss', never as in 'treasure'
sh	as in 'ship'
ch	as in 'chew'
dj	as the 'j' in 'jaw'
th	as the 'th' in 'lather'
ng	as in 'sing'
ngn	as the meeting of sounds in 'hang-nail'
rr	a trilled 'r'
rt	as the 'rt' in American English 'start'
rd	as the 'rd' in American English 'weird'
rn	as the 'rn' in American English 'earn'
rl	as the 'rl' in American English 'earl'
dn	as the 'dn' in 'hadn't'
dl	as the 'dl' in 'saddle'

Language Difficulties

Do you speak English?	Snakker du engelsk?
	snah-kehrr du *ehng*-ehlsk?
Does anyone here speak English?	Er det noen som snakker engelsk her?
	Ehrr day *noo*-ehn sohm *snah*-kehrr *ehng*-ehlsk harr?
I (don't) understand.	Jeg forstår (ikke).
	yay for-*stohrr* (*i*-keh).
I speak a little Norwegian.	Jeg snakker litt norsk.
	yay *snah*-kehrr lit noshk.
What does ... mean?	Hva betyr ...?
	vah bö-*türr* ...?

How do you say ...?	Hvordan sier du? *voorr*-dahn *see*-ehrr doo?	
Could you repeat that?	Kan du gjenta det? kahn du *yehn*-tah day?	
Could you speak slower?	Kan du snakke langsommere? kahn du *snah*-keh *lahng*-sohm-eh-rreh?	
Could you write it down?	Kan du skrive det? kahn du *skree*-veh day?	

Greetings

Hello.	Goddag. gud-*dahg*.
Good morning.	God morgen. goo *morn*.
Good afternoon.	Goddag. goo-*dahg*.
Good evening/night.	God kveld/natt. goo *kvehl*/*naht*.
Goodbye.	Ha det. *hah*-day.
How are you?	Hvordan har du det? *voorr*-dahn *hahrr* du day?
Well, thanks.	Bra, takk. brrah tahk.

Titles

Madam/Mrs/Ms	fru	frroo
Miss	frøken	*frrer*-kehn
Sir/Mr	herr	harr

Introductions

What is your name?	Hva heter du?
	vah *hay*-tehrr du?
My name is ...	Jeg heter ...
	yai *hay*-tehrr ...
I'd like to introduce you to ...	Dette er ...
	deh-teh arr ...
I'm pleased to meet you.	Hyggelig å treffe deg.
	her-geh-lee oh *trreh*-feh dai.

Fast Talk

It's considered good manners to shake hands with Norwegians when you meet. Remember, this includes both men and women; many Norwegian women feel ignored in English-speaking nations where usually only the men shake hands.

After having met a few times, a friendly hug or a peck on the cheek is common – this includes both women and men.

Personal Details

Do you have a boyfriend/girlfriend?	Har du kjæreste?
	hahrr du *cha*-rreh-steh?
Are you married?	Er du gift?
	arr du *yift*?

PHRASE BUILDER

I'm ...	Jeg er ...	yai arr ...
divorced	skilt	shilt
in a relationship	i et forhold	ee eht *fohrr*-hold
separated	separert	seh-pah-*rrehrt*
single	enslig	ehn-shlee
married	gift	*yift*

My husband is here.	Min mannen er her. min *muhn-n* arr harr.
My wife is here.	Mi kone er her. mi koo-nö arr harr.
Do you have children?	Har du barn? hahrr du *bahrrn*?
I have a daughter/son.	Jeg har en datter/sønn. yai hahrr ehn *dah*-tehrr/sern.
Where are you from?	Hvor er du fra? voorr *arr* du frrah?

PHRASE BUILDER

I'm from ...	Jeg er fra ...	yai *arr* frrah ...
Australia	Australia	ow-*strrah*-lee-ah
Canada	Canada	*kah*-nah-dah
England	England	*ehng*-lahn
Ireland	Irland	*eerr*-lahn
New Zealand	New Zealand	nü see-lahn
the USA	USA	oo-ehss-*ah*

Age

How old are you?	Hvor gammel er du? voor *gah*-mehl arr du?
I'm ... years old.	Jeg er ... yai arr ...
Happy birthday!	Gratulerer med dagen! grah-tü-*leh*-rrehrr may *dah*-gehn!
How old is he/she?	Hvor gammel er han/hun? voorr *gah*-mehl arr hahn/hun?
He/She is ... years old.	Han/hun er ... Hahn/hun arr ...

Occupations & Study

What do you do?	Hva driver du med?	
	vah drree-vehrr du may?	
I work in ...	Jeg jobber i ...	
	yai jo-behrr ee ...	
health care		helsevesenet
		hehl-seh-vay-seh-neh
IT		IT
		ee-tay
marketing		markedsføring
		mahrr-kehds-fer-ing
What are you studying?	Hva studerer du?	
	vah stoo-*deh*-rrehrr du?	
I'm studying ...	Jeg studerer ...	
	yai stoo-*deh*-rrehrr ...	
art		kunst
		kunst
business		foretnings
		fo-*rreht*-nings
history		historie
		hi-stoo-rree-eh
science		vitenskaps
		vee-tön-skahps

PHRASE BUILDER

I'm a/an ...	Jeg er ...	yai *arr* ...
office worker	kontor-arbeider	koon-*toorr*-ahrr-bai-dehrr
student	student	stoo-*dehnt*
teacher	lærer	*la*-rrehrr
tradesperson	arbeider	ahrr-*bai*-dehrr
writer	forfatter	forr-*faht*-tehrr

CHATTING & BASICS

15

Interests

What do you do in your spare time?	Hva gjør du i fritiden? vah yer-rr du ee frree-tee-dehn?
What sport do you play?	Hva slags idrett driver du? vah shluhgs id-rreht drri-vehrr du?
Do you like ...?	Liker du ...? lee-kehrr du ...?
I (don't) like ...	Jeg liker (ikke) ... yai lee-kehrr (i-keh) ...
cooking	matlaging *maht-lah*-ging
football/ soccer	fotball *foot*-bahl
going to the cinema	gå på kino goh poh *chee*-noo
music	musikk moo-*sik*
photography	fotografering foo-too-grrah-*fay*-rring
shopping	å handle oh *hahnd*-leh
travelling	å reiser oh *rrai*-seh

Feelings

I feel cold/hot.	Jeg fryser/Jeg er varm. yai *frrü*-sehrr/yai arr *vahrrm*.
I'm in a hurry.	Jeg har det travelt. yai hahrr day *trah*-vehlt.
I (don't) like you.	Jeg liker deg (ikke). yai *lee*-kehrr dai (i-keh).

PHRASE BUILDER

I'm ...	Jeg er ...	*yai arr ...*
angry	sinna	*si*-nah
grateful	takknemlig	*tahk-nehm*-li
happy	lykkelig	*lü*-keh-lee
hungry	sulten	*suhl*-tehn
tired	trøtt	trrert
sad	trist	*trrist*
sleepy	søvnig	*serv*-nee
thirsty	tørst	tersht
well	bra	brrah
worried	urolig	oo-*rroo*-lee

I'm sorry. (condolence)	Kondolerer. kohn-doo-*leh*-rrehrr.	
You're right.	Du har rett. du hahrr *rreht*.	

Numbers

0	null	nool
1	en	ehn
2	to	too
3	tre	trray
4	fire	*fee*-rreh
5	fem	fehm
6	seks	sehks
7	sju/syv	shu/süv
8	åtte	*oh*-teh
9	ni	nee
10	ti	tee

11	elleve	*ehl*-veh
12	tolv	tol
13	tretten	*trreh*-tehn
14	fjorten	*fyor*-tehn
15	femten	*fehm*-tehn
16	seksten	*sehks*-tehn
17	sytten	*sü*-tehn
18	atten	*ah*-tehn
19	nitten	*ni*-tehn
20	tjue	*choo*-eh
21	tjueen	choo-eh-*ehn*
30	tretti/tredve	*trreh*-tee/*trrehd*-veh
40	førti	*fer*-rr-tee
50	femti	*fehm*-tee
60	seksti	*sehks*-tee
70	sytti	*ser*-tee
80	åtti	*oh*-tee
90	nitti	*ni*-tee
100	hundre	*hun*-drreh
1000	tusen	*too*-sehn
one million	en million	ehn mi-lee-*yoon*

USEFUL WORDS

once	en gang	ehn guhng
twice	to ganger	*too* guhng-örr
few	få	for
many	mange	*muhng*-ö
more	mer/flere	may-rr/*flay*-rrö
too much	for mye	forr *mü*-yö

Time

What date is it today?	Hvilken dato er det i dag? vil-kehn *dah*-toh arr day ee *dahg*?
What time is it?	Hva er klokka? vah arr *klo*-kah?
It's ...	Klokka er ... klo-kah arr ...
in the morning	om formiddagen orm *forr*-mi-dah-gehn
in the afternoon	om ettermiddagen orm *eh*-tehrr-mi-dah-gehn
in the evening	om kvelden orm *kvehl*-n
Quarter past (one)	Kvart over (ett) kvahrrt *oh*-vehrr (eht)
Twenty past one.	Ti på halv to (lit: ten to half two) tee poh hahl too
Half past one.	Halv to (lit: half two) hahl too
Twenty to (one)	Ti over halv (ett) tee *oh*-vehrr hahl (eht)
Quarter to (one)	Kvart på (ett) kvahrrt poh (ett)
At what time?	Når? nohrr?
At ...	Klokka ... klo-kah ...

Days of the Week

Monday	mandag	*mahn*-dah(g)
Tuesday	tirsdag	*teesh*-dah(g)
Wednesday	onsdag	*uns*-dah(g)
Thursday	torsdag	*toosh*-dah(g)
Friday	fredag	*frray*-dah(g)
Saturday	lørdag	*ler*-rr-dah(g)
Sunday	søndag	*sern*-dah(g)

Months

January	januar	yay-noo-*ahrr*
February	februar	feh-brroo-*ahrr*
March	mars	mahsh
April	april	ah-*prreel*
May	mai	mai
June	juni	*yoo*-nee
July	juli	*yoo*-lee
August	august	ow-*gust*
September	september	sehp-*tehm*-behrr
October	oktober	uk-*too*-behrr
November	november	noh-*vehm*-behrr
December	desember	deh-*sehm*-behrr

Present

now	nå
	noh
today	i dag
	ee-*dahg*

this morning	i morges i-*morr*-ös
tonight (evening)	i kveld i-*kvehl*
this week	denne uka deh-neh *oo*-kah
this year	i år i-*yor*-rr

Past

yesterday	i går i-*gor*-rr
day before yesterday	i forgårs i *forr*-gor-sh
yesterday morning	i går formiddag i-*gor*-rr *forr*-mid-dahg
last night	i natt i-*naht*
last week	forrige uke *for*-rree-yeh oo-keh
last month	forrige måned *for*-rree-yeh *mor*-nehd
last year	i fjor ee-*fyoorr*

Future

tomorrow (morning)	i morgen ee-*mor*-rrn
day after tomorrow	i overmorgen ee-*oh*-vehrr-mor-rrn
next week/year	neste uke/år *neh*-steh oo-keh/or-rr

Weather

What's the weather forecast?	Hva er værmeldinga?	vah arr *varr*-meh-ling-ah?

Will it be ... ?	Blir det ... ?	bleerr day ... ?
cold	kaldt	kahlt
warm/hot	varmt	vah-rmt
raining	regn	rrain
snowing	snø	sner
sunny	mye sol	mü-yö *sool*
windy	mye vind	mü-yö *vin*

Directions

Where is ...?	Hvor er ...?	*voor* arr ...?
Which way is ...?	Hvilken retning er ...?	vil-kehn reht-ning arr ... ?
How do I get to ...?	Hvordan kommer jeg til ...?	voor-dahn ko-mehrr yai til ...?
Is it far from here?	Er det langt herfra?	arr day *lahngt harr*-frrah?
Can you show me (on the map)?	Kan du vise meg (på kartet)?	kahn du vee-seh mai (poh *kahrr*-teh)?
Can I walk there?	Kan jeg gå dit?	kahn yai *goh* deet?
Are there other means of getting there?	Er det en annen måte å komme dit på?	arr deh ehn *ahn*-ön mor-tö or kom-mö *deet* po?
behind	bak	bak

Go straight ahead.	Det er rett fram.	deh arr *rreht* frruhm.
Turn left at the ...	Ta til venstre ved ...	*tah* til *vehn*-streh vay ...
Turn right at the ...	Ta til høyre ved ...	*tah* til *höü*-rreh vay ...
next corner	neste hjørne	*neh*-steh *yer-rr*-neh
traffic lights	lyskrysset	*lüs*-krrü-seh
It's two blocks down.	Det er to kvartal videre.	deh arr *too* kvuh-*rtahl vee*-dö-rrö.

in front of	foran	fo-*rruhn*
far	langt	luhngt
near	nær	narr
opposite	overfor	*or*-vörr-*forr*
next to	ved siden av	*veh*-si-dehn-*uhv*
north	nå	noh
south	sør	ser-rr
east	øst	öst
west	vest	vehst

CHATTING & BASICS

23

Transport

≡ Fast Phrases

One ticket to ... please.	En billett til...takk. ehn bi-leht til...tahk.
When's the next (bus)?	Når går neste (buss)? Norr gorr neh-steh (bus)?
I want to get off in/at ...	Jeg vil gå av i/på ... yai vil goh ahv ee/poh ...

At the Airport

Is there a flight to ...?	Er det et fly til ...? arr day eht flü til ...?
How long does the flight take?	Hvor lang tid tar flyvningen? voor *lahng* tee tahrr *flüv*-ning-ehn?
What is the flight number?	Hva er flightnummeret? vah arr *flait*-nu-mö-rreh?
boarding pass	ombordstigningskort ohm-*boorr*-steeg-nings-kort
airport tax	lufthavnavgift *luft*-hahven-*ahv*-yift

Buying Tickets

Where can I buy a ticket?	Hvor kan jeg kjøpe billett? *voor* kahn yai *cher*-peh bi-*leht?*
I want to go to ...	Jeg skal til ... yai skahl til ...
Do I need to book a seat?	Er det nødvendig å bestille plass? arr day nerd-*vehn*-dee oh be-*sti*-leh plahs?
I'd like to book a seat to ...	Jeg vil gjerne bestille sitte-plass til ... yai vil *yarr*-neh be-*sti*-leh si-teh-plahs til ...
Is it completely full?	Er det helt fullt? arr day *haylt* foolt?

PHRASE BUILDER

I'd like ...	Jeg vil gjerne ha ... yai vil *yarr*-neh hah ...	
a one-way ticket	enkelt billett	*ehn*-kehlt-bi-*leht*
a return ticket	tur-retur	*too*-rray-*toorr*
two tickets	to billetter	too bi-*leh*-tehrr
tickets for all of us	billetter til oss alle sammen	bi-*leh*-tehrr til os *ah*-leh *sah*-mehn
a student's fare	student-billett	stoo-*dehnt*-bi-*leht*
a child's fare	barnebillett	*bahrr*-neh-bi-*leht*
a senior's fare	honnør-billett	hoh-*ner*-rr-bi-*leht*
1st class	første klasse	*fersh*-teh klah-seh
economy	økonomi	er-*koh*-noh-mee

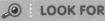

LOOK FOR

ANKOMST	ARRIVALS
AVGANG	DEPARTURES
BAGASJE	LUGGAGE PICKUP
BILLETTKONTOR	TICKET OFFICE
JERNBANESTASJON	TRAIN STATION
INFORMASJON	INFORMATION
INNSJEKKING	CHECK-IN
RESERVERT	RESERVED
RUTEPLAN	TIMETABLE
SPOR	PLATFORM
TOLL	CUSTOMS
WC/TOALETTER	TOILETS

Can I get a stand-by ticket?	Kan jeg få en sjansebillett? kahn yai foh ehn *shahn*-seh-bi-*leht*?
How long does the trip take?	Hvor lenge tar reisa? voor *lehng*-eh tahrr *rrai*-suh?
Is it a direct route?	Er det direkte rute? arr day di-*rrehk*-teh roo-teh?

Bicycle

Where can I hire a bicycle?	Hvor kan jeg leie en sykkel? *voor* kahn yai *lai*-eh ehn *sü*-kehl?
Do you have a helmet?	Har du hjelm? hahrr du *yehlm*?

Bus

Where is the bus/ tram stop?	Hvor er bussholdeplassen/ trikkholdeplassen? voor arr *bus*-hoh-leh-plah-sehn/ *trrik*-hoh-leh-plah-sehn?
Does this bus go to ...?	Går denne bussen til ...? gorr deh-neh *bus*-ehn til ...?
Which bus goes to ...?	Hvilken buss går til ...? *vil*-kehn bus gorr til ...?

Car & Motorbike

Where's the next petrol station?	Hvor er nærmeste bensinstasjon? voor arr *narr*-meh-steh behn-seen-stah-*shoon*?
How long can I park here?	Hvor lenge kan bilen min stå her? voorr *lehng*-eh kahn *bee*-lehn meen stoh harr?
Does this road lead to ...?	Er dette veien til ...? arr deh-teh *vai*-ehn til ...?
The battery is flat.	Batteriet er flatt. bah-teh-*rree*-eh arr flaht.
I have a flat tyre.	Hjulet er punktert. *yoo*-leh arr poong-*tayrt*.

It's not working.	Det fungerer ikke. day foon-*gay*-rrehrr i-keh.
air (for tyres)	luft luft
battery	batteri bah-teh-*rree*
brakes	bremser *brrehm*-sehrr
clutch	kløtsj klerch
driver's licence	førerkort *fer*-rrehrr-kort
engine	motor *moh*-torr
lights	lykter *lük*-tehrr
puncture	punktering poong-*tay*-rring
radiator	radiator rrah-dee-*ah*-toorr
road map	kart kahrt
tyres	dekk dehk
windscreen	frontrute *frront*-rroo-teh
I need a mechanic.	Jeg trenger bilmekaniker. yai *trrehng*-ehrr *beel*-meh-*kah*-ni-kehrr.

Taxi

Where can I get hold of a taxi?	Hvor kan jeg få tak i en drosje? *vorr kahn yai foh tahk ee ehn drro-sheh?*
Please take me to ...	Vil du kjøre meg til ...? *vil du cher-rreh mai til ...?*
How much does it cost to go to ...?	Hvor mye koster det å kjøre til ...? *voorr mü-eh ko-stehrr day oh cher-rreh til ...?*
Here is fine, thank you.	Du kan stoppe her, takk. *du kahn sto-peh harr tuhk.*
Continue!	Bare fortsett! *bah-rreh fort-seht!*
The next street to the left/right.	Neste gate til venstre/høyre. *neh-steh gah-teh til vehn-streh/höü-rreh.*
Stop here!	Stopp her! *stop harr!*
Please slow down.	Vær så snill og kjør litt saktere. *varr shoo snil oh cher-rr lit sahk-teh-rreh.*
Please wait here.	Vær så snill å vente her. *varr shoo snil oh vehn-teh harr.*

Train

Is this the right platform for ...?	Er dette riktig spor for toget til ...? *arr deh-teh rik-tee spoorr forr toh-geh til ...?*
The train leaves from platform ...	Toget går fra spor ... *toh-geh gorr frrah spoorr ...*

🔊 LISTEN FOR

The train is delayed.	Toget er forsinket toh-geh arr for-*shing*-keht
The train is cancelled.	Toget er innstilt. toh-geh arr *in*-stilt
Passengers must ...	Reisende må ... *rrai*-seh-deh moh ...
change trains	bytte tog *būt*-teh tohg
change platforms	gå til spor ... *goh* til spoorr ...

Which line takes me to ...?	Hvilken linje/bane må jeg ta til ...? *vil*-kehn *lin*-yeh/*bah*-neh moh yai tah til ...?
Is that seat taken?	Er denne plassen opptatt? arr *deh*-neh *plah*-sehn op-taht?
What is the next station?	Hva er neste stasjon? vah arr *neh*-ste stah-*shoon*?
dining car	spisevogn *spee*-seh-vogn
express	ekspresstog ehks-*prrehs*-tohg
local	lokaltog loo-*kahl*-tohg
sleeping car	sovevogn *soh*-veh-vogn

Accommodation

⩶ Fast Phrases

I have a reservation.	Jeg har en reservasjon. *yai hahrr ehn reh-sehrr-vah-shoon.*
What time is checkout?	Når er utsjekk? *Norr arr oot-shehk?*
I'm leaving now/ tomorrow.	Jeg reiser nå/i morgen. *yai rai-sehrr noh/ee-morrn.*

Finding Accommodation

PHRASE BUILDER

Where is a ...?	Hvor er et ...?	*voorr arr eht ...?*
cheap hotel	billig hotell	*bi-lee hoh-tehl*
good hotel	godt hotell	*guht hoh-tehl*
nearby hotel	hotell i nærheten	*hoh-tehl ee narr-haytn*
nice/ quaint hotel	koselig/ gammel-dags hotell	*koo-shlee/ gah-mehl-dahgs hoh-tehl*

Booking & Checking In

Do you have any rooms available?	Har du ledige rom?	hahrr du *lay*-dee-eh rrum?
There are (four) of us.	Vi er (fire) stykker.	vee arr *(fee*-rreh) stü-kehrr.
How much is it per night/per person?	Hvor mye er det pr. dag/pr. person?	voor *mü*-eh arr day parr *dahg*/parr parr-s*hoon*?
Is there a reduction for students/children?	Gir du studentrabatt/barnerabatt?	yeerr du stoo-*dehnt*-rrah-*baht*/*bahrr*-neh-rrah-*baht*?
I'm going to stay for ...	Jeg har tenkt å bli her ...	yai hahrr *tehngkt* oh blee harr ...
one day	en dag	*ehn dahg*
two days	to dager	*too dah*-gehrr
one week	en uke	ehn *oo*-keh

PHRASE BUILDER

I'd like a ...	Jeg vil gjerne ha...	yay vil *yarr*-neh hah...
single room	et enkeltrom	eht *ehng*-kehlt-rrum
double room	et dobbeltrom	eht *do*-behlt-rrum
dorm bed	seng på sovesal	sehng poh *soh*-veh-sahl
bathroom	bad	bahd
shower	dusj	doosh
television	tv	tay-vay
window	vindu	*vin*-doo

🔍 LOOK FOR

GJESTGIVERI/PENSJONAT	GUESTHOUSE
KAMPING/LEIRPLASS	CAMPING GROUND
LEDIG	VACANCY
VANDRERHJEM	YOUTH HOSTEL

Does it include breakfast?	Inkluderer det frokosten?	in-kloo-*day*-rrehrr day *froo*-kostn?
Where/when is breakfast served?	Hvor/når er frokost servert?	voorr/norr arr *frroo*-kost sarr-*varrt*?
Can I see it?	Kan jeg få se det?	kahn yai foh *say* day?
Are there any cheaper rooms?	Har du billigere rom?	hahrr du *bi*-lee-eh-rreh rrum?
I don't like this room.	Jeg liker ikke dette rommet.	yai *lee*-kehrr i-keh deh-teh *rrum*-eh.
Are there any others?	Har du andre?	hahrr du *ahn*-drreh?

🔊 LISTEN FOR

Sorry, we're full.	Beklager, det er fullt.	beh-*klah*-gehrr day arr *fült*
It's ... per day/per person.	Det er ... pr. dag/pr. person.	day arr ... parr *dahg*/parr parr-*shoon*
Do you have identification?	Har du legitimasjon?	hahrr du lay-gi-ti-mah-shoon?
How many nights?	Hvor mange netter?	voorr mahng-eh *neh*-tehrr?
How long will you be staying?	Hvor lenge blir du her?	voorr *lehng*-eh *blee*rr du harr?

33

It's ...	Det er ... day arr ...
expensive	dyrt *dürt*
noisy	for mye bråk forr *mü*-eh brrork
too dark	for mørkt forr *mer-rrt*
too small	for lite fo *lee*-teh
It's fine, I'll take it.	Bra, jeg tar det. brrah yai *tahrr* day
I'm not sure how long I'm staying.	Jeg vet ikke hvor lenge jeg skal bli her. yai *veht i*-keh voorr *lehng*-eh yai skahl blee harr.
Is there a lift?	Finnes det en heis her? fins day ehn *hais* harr?
What is the address?	Hva er adressen? vah arr uh-*drreh*-sehn?
Could you write the address, please?	Kan du være så snill å skrive opp adressen? kahn du *va*-rreh soh snil oh *skree*-veh op ah-*dreh*-sehn?

Requests

Do you have a safe where I can leave my valuables?	Har du en safe der jeg kan legge verdisakene mine? hahrr du ehn sayf darr yai kahn *leh*-geh varr-*dee*-sah-keh-neh *mee*-neh?
Where is the bathroom?	Hvor er badet? voorr arr *bah*-deh?

Is there somewhere to wash clothes?	Kan jeg vaske klærne mine noe sted?
	kahn yai vah-skeh klarr-neh *mee*-neh *noo*-eh *steh?*
Can I use the kitchen?	Er det lov å bruke kjøkkenet?
	arr day lohv *oh* brroo-keh cher-keh-neh?
Please wake me up at ...	Vær så snill å vekke meg ...
	varr shoo snil oh veh-keh *mai* ...
Can I use the telephone?	Kan jeg få låne telefonen?
	kahn yai foh loh-neh *teh-leh-*foo-nehn?
The room needs to be cleaned.	Dette rommet bør gjøres reint.
	deh-teh rru-meh *ber-rr* yer-rrehs rraynt.
Please change the sheets.	Vær så snill å skifte sengetøy.
	varr shoo snil oh shif-teh sehng-eh-töy.
I've locked myself out of my room.	Jeg har låst meg ute av rommet mitt.
	yai hahrr lohst *mai* oo-teh *ahv* rru-meh *mit.*
The toilet won't flush.	Jeg får ikke spylt ned på toalettet.
	yai forr i-keh spült *nay poh* too-a-leht-teh.

Useful Words - Accommodation

name	nahvn
	nuhvn
surname	etternavn
	*eh-*tehrr-nahvn
address	adresse
	*ah-*drrehs-seh

35

room number	romnummer *rrum*-noom-ehrr
air-conditioning	klimaanlegg *klee*-mah-ahn-lehg
balcony	balkong buhl-*kong*
bathroom	bad bahd
bed	seng sehng
bill	regning *rrai*-ning
blanket	teppe *teh*-peh
chair	stol stool
clean	rein rrain
cold	kaldt kahlt
cupboard	skap skahp
dirty	skitten *shit*-n
double bed	dobbeltseng *do*-behlt-sehng
electricity	strøm strrerm
fan	vifte *vif*-tö
hot	varmt *vahrrmt*

key	nøkkel	*ner*-kehl
lift (elevator)	heis	hais
light bulb	lyspære	*lüs*-pa-rrö
a lock	lås	lors
mattress	madrass	mah-*drrahs*
mirror	speil	spail
padlock	hengelås	*hehng*-eh-lors
pillow	pute	*poo*-teh
quiet	stille	*sti*-leh
room (in hotel)	rom/værelse	rrum/*varr*-ehl-seh
sheet	laken	*lah*-kehn
soap	såpe	*soh*-peh
suitcase	koffert	*koh*-fört
swimming pool (indoor)	svømmehall	*sver*-meh-hahl
table	bord	boorr
toilet	do	doo

toilet paper	dopapir
	doo-pah-*peerr*
towel	håndkle
	hohn-klay
water	vann
	vahn

Camping

Am I allowed to camp here?	Er camping tillatt her?
	arr *kam*-ping *ti*-laht harr?
Is there a campsite nearby?	Finnes det en camping-plass i nærheten?
	fins day ehn *kam*-ping plahs ee *narr-hay*-tehn?

Useful Words - Camping

tent	telt
	tehlt
sleeping bag	sovepose
	soh-veh-*poo*-seh
crampons	brodder
	brruh-dör
firewood	ved
	vay
gas cartridge	propanbeholder
	prroo-*pahn*-beh-*hoh*-lehrr
ice axe	isøks
	ees-erks
stove	kokeplater
	koo-keh-*plah*-tehrr

Eating & Drinking

≋ Fast Phrases

Table for ..., please.	Et bord til ..., takk.
	eht *boo-rr* til ... tahk.
I'd like (a beer), please.	Kan jeg få (en øl), takk.
	kahn yai foh ehn erl tahk.
Please bring the bill.	Kan jeg få regningen, takk.
	kahn yai foh *rrai*-ning-ehn *tahk*?

Meals

breakfast	frokost
	frroo-kost
lunch	lunsj
	lernsh
dinner	middag
	mid-dahg
a snack	mellommåltid
	meh-lohm-mohl-tee

Ordering & Paying

Are you still serving food?	Serverer dere fortsatt mat?
	sehrr-*vehrr*-ehrr *dehrr*-eh *fort*-saht maht?

Do you have a reservation?	Har du/dere en reservasjon? hahrr doo/*deh*-rre ehn reh-sehrr-vah-*shoon*
Come back at (8pm).	Kom tilbake klokka (åtte). kohm til-*bah*-keh klok-kah *oh*-teh

Can I see the menu please?	Kan jeg få menyen, takk. kahn yai foh meh-*nüy*-ehn tahk.
What does it include?	Hva inkluderer det? vah in-kloo-*deh*-rreh day?
What would you recommend?	Hva anbefaler du? vah *ahn*-beh-fah-lehrr doo?
I'll have this, please.	Jeg vil gjerne ha denne. yai vil *yehrr*-neh hah deh-neh.
Not too spicy please.	Ikke for sterkt krydra, takk. i-keh forr *shtehrrkt* krrü-drrah tahk.
I didn't order this.	Jeg bestilte ikke dette. yai beh-*stil*-teh i-keh deh-teh.
That was delicious.	Det var nydelig. Day vahrr *nü*-deh-lee.
I'd like to pay the bill.	Kan jeg få regningen, takk. kahn yai foh *rrai*-ning-ehn *tahk*?
✂ **Bill, please!**	Regningen, takk! *rrai*-ning-ehn, tahk!
Is service included in the bill?	Er bevertninga iberegnet? arr bö-*vart*-ning-uh *ee*-bö-rray-nöt?

Utensils

Please bring...	Kan du ta med ... kahn doo tah may ...

an ashtray	askebeger
	ahs-keh-bay-görr
a cup	en kopp
	ehn *kop*
a drink	en drink
	ehn *drringk*
a fork	en gaffel
	ehn *gahf*-ehl
a glass	et glass
	eht *glahs*

Local Knowledge

Restaurants

Where would you go for ...	Hvor vil du anbefale for...
	vohrr vil doo ahn-beh-fah-leh forr...
local specialities?	lokale spesialiteter?
	loh-*kah*-leh
	speh-see-ahl-ee-*tay*-tehrr?
a celebration?	å feire?
	oh *fai*-rreh?
a cheap meal?	en billig måltid?
	ehn *bi*-lee *mohl*-tee?
Can you recommend a ...	Kan du anbefale en ...
	kahn doo ahn-beh-fah-leh ehn ...
bar	bar
	bahrr
cafe	cafe
	kah-*fay*
dish	rett
	reht
restaurant	restaurant
	reh-stau-rrang

41

a knife	en kniv
	ehn *kneev*
a plate	en tallerken
	ehn tahl-*lehrr*-kehn
a spoon	en skje
	ehn *shay*

Special Diets & Allergies

I'm vegetarian.	Jeg er vegetarianer.
	yai arr veh-geh-tah-rri-*ah-nehrr*.
I'm vegan.	Jeg er veganer.
	yai arr vay-*gah*-nerr.
I don't eat meat.	Jeg spiser ikke kjøtt.
	yai *spee*-sehrr i-keh chert.
I don't eat chicken or fish or ham.	Jeg spiser verken kylling eller fisk eller skinke.
	yai *spee*-sehr *vehrr*-kehn *chü*-ling eh-lehrr *fisk* eh-lerr *shing*-keh.
I'm allergic to (nuts).	Jeg er allergisk mot (nøtter).
	yai ehrr ah-*lehrr*-gisk moot (*ner*-tehrr).

PHRASE BUILDER

Could you prepare a meal without ...?	Kan du lage et måltid uten ...?	kahn doo lah-geh eht mohl-tee oo-tehn ...?
dairy	meieri	*mai*-eh-rree
eggs	egg	ehg
gluten	gluten	gloo-ten
meat stock	kjøttkraft	chert-krrahft
seafood	sjømat	sher-maht

In the Bar

I'll buy you a drink.	Jeg spanderer en drink. yai spahn-*deh*-rrehrr ehn *drrink*.
What would you like?	Hva vil du ha? vah vil doo hah?
I'll have ...	Jeg vil gjerne ha ... yai vil *yarr*-neh hah
Same again, please.	Det samme igjen, takk. day *sah*-meh ee-*yehn* tahk.
Cheers!	Skål! skohl!

Drinks (non-alcoholic)

cocoa	kakao kah-*kow*
coffee	kaffe *kah*-feh
cola	cola *koo*-la
fruit juice	jus yoos
ice	is ees
milk	melk mehlk
mineral water	farris *fahrr*-is
non-alcoholic	alkoholfri *ahl*-koh-*hool*-frree
squash	saft sahft

tea	te
	tay
water	vann
	vahn

Alcoholic Drinks

beer	øl
	erl
brandy	brennevin
	brrehn-eh-veen
dark beer	bayer
	bah-yehrr
double	dobbel
	dor-behl
liqueur	likør
	li-*ker*-rr
port	portvin
	purrt-veen
red/white wine	rødvin/hvitvin
	rrer-veen/*veet*-vin
rum	rom
	rroom
sparkling	musserende
	mus-*sehr*-ehn-eh

Menu Decoder

Staple Foods & Condiments

egg ehg eggs
fisk fisk fish
fløte *fler*-teh cream
frukt frrukt fruit
grønnsaker *grrern*-suh-kehrr vegetables
grovbrød *grrohv*-brrer brown bread
kjøtt chert meat
loff loof white bread
melk mehlk milk
ost ust cheese
pepper *peh*-pehrr pepper
rømme *rrer*-mö sour cream
sennep *sehn*-ehp mustard
smør smer-rr butter
sukker *su*-kehrr sugar

Frokost / Breakfast

bløtkokt *blert*-kukt soft-boiled
eggerøre *ehg*-eh-*rrer*-rreh scrambled eggs

grøt grrert porridge, cereal
hardkokt *hahrr*-kukt hard-boiled
havregrøt hah-vrreh-*grrert* oatmeal porridge
havrekjeks hah-vrreh-*chehks* oatmeal biscuits
helkornbrød *hehl*-koorrn-brrer wholemeal bread
honning *hun*-ning honey
kavring *kah*-vrring rusk
kjeks chehks biscuit
knekkebrød *kneh*-keh-brrer crisp-bread
pålegg *poh*-lehg food on top of a sandwich, like cold cuts
peanøttsmør *pee-ah*-nert-smer-rr peanut butter
rundstykke *rrun*-stü-keh roll
skive *shee*-veh slice
smørbrød smer-brrer open sandwich
speilegg *spayl*-ehg fried egg (sunny side up)
spekeskinke *spay*-keh-shin-keh cured ham
syltetøy *sül*-teh-töy jam

45

Kjøtt / Meat

and ahn duck
gås gors goose
kalkun kahl-koon turkey
kalvekjøtt kahl-veh-chert veal
kjøttbolle chert-bor-leh
meatball
kylling chül-ling chicken
mørbrad mer-brrahd rump
steak
nyre nü-rreh kidney
oksekjøtt uk-seh-chert beef
pølse perl-seh sausage
reinsdyrstek rrains-dehrr-stayk
roast reindeer
sauekjøtt sow-eh-chert lamb/
mutton
skinke shin-keh ham
svinekjøtt svee-neh-chert pork
vaktel vahk-tehl quail

Sjømat / Seafood

ål ohl eel
ansjos ahn-shoos anchovy
blåskjell blor-shehl mussel
brisling brris-ling sprat/sardine
hyse/kolje hü-seh/korl-yeh
haddock
flyndre flün-drreh flounder
hummer hu-mehrr lobster
kryddersild/sursild krrüd-ehrr-sil/surr-sil pickled/marinated
herring
kreps krrehps crayfish
laks lahks salmon
makrell mah-krrehl mackerel
reker rray-kehrr shrimps

sei say coalfish
sild sil herring
sjøørret sher-er-rreht sea trout
sjøtunge sher-tun-geh sole
steinbit stayn-bit catfish
torsk torshk cod
tunfisk toon-fisk tuna

Frukt / Fruit

ananas ah-nah-nahs pineapple
appelsin ah-pehl-seen orange
aprikos ah-prree-koos apricot
banan bah-nahn banana
bjørnebær byer-neh-barr
blackberries
blåbær bloh-barr bilberries
bringebær brring-eh-barr
raspberries
druer drroo-ehrr grapes
eple ehp-leh apple
fersken fehrrsh-kehn peach
fruktsalat frrukt-sah-laht fruit
salad
jordbær yoorr-barr
strawberries
kirsebær shi-sheh-barr cherry
korint kor-int currant
pære pa-rreh pear
plomme plu-meh plum
rabarbra rruh-buhrr-brruh
rhubarb
rips rrips redcurrants
rosin rroo-sin raisin
sitron si-trroon lemon
solbær sool-barr blackcurrants
stikkelsbær sti-kehls-barr
gooseberries
tyttebær tü-teh-barr cranberries

Grønnsaker/ Vegetables

agurk ah-*gurrk* cucumber
blomkål *blorm*-korl cauliflower
bønner *bern*-nehrr beans
erter *ahrr*-tehrr peas
gresskar *grrehs*-kahrr marrow/ squash
gressløk *grrehs*-lerk chives
gulrøtter *gu*-leh-rrer-tehrr carrots
kål korl cabbage
kålrabi korl-*rah*-bi swede
linser *lin*-sehrr lentils
løk lerk onion
lompe *lum*-peh potato pancake
pepperrot *peh*-pehrr-*rroot* horseradish
potetmos por-*teht*-mos mashed potatoes
purre *pu*-rreh leek
raspeballer *rrah*-speh-*bah*-lehrr potato dumplings
reddik *rreh*-dik radish
rødbeter rrer-*bay*-tehrr beetroot

rødkål *rrer*-korl red cabbage
rosenkål *rroo*-sehn-*korl* Brussels sprouts
sjampinjong sham-pin-*yong* button mushroom
sopp sop mushroom
spinat spi-*naht* spinach
sylteagurk *sül*-teh-ah-*gurrk* pickled gherkin
tomat too-*maht* tomato

Dessert

eplekake *eh*-pleh-*kah*-keh apple cake
is ees ice cream
kake *kah*-keh cake
marengs mah-*rrehngs* meringue
pannekake *pah*-neh-*kah*-keh pancake
sjokolade shoo-koo-*lah*-deh chocolate
småkake *smor*-kah-keh biscuit/ cookie
sukkerbrød *suk*-kehrr-*brrer* sponge cake
terte *tehrr*-teh tart

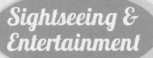

Sightseeing & Entertainment

≡ Fast Phrases

What time does it open/close?	Når åpner/stenger den? norr *orp*-nehrr/*stehng*-ehrr dehn?
Can I take photographs?	Kan jeg ta bilder? *kahn* yai tah *bil*-dehrr?
Is there a local entertainment guide?	Finnes det en lokalunderholdningsguide? fins day ehn loo-*kahl*-oo-nehrr-*hohl*-nings-gaid?

Planning

Do you have a guidebook/ local map?	Har du en guidebok/et lokalkart? hah du ehn *gaid-book*/eht *lo-kahl*-kahrt?
What are the main attractions?	Hva er de viktigste severdigheter? vah arr dee *vik*-teeg-steh say-*varr*-dee-hay-tehrr?
I have (one) day.	Jeg har (en) dag. yai hahrr (ehn) dahg.
I'd like to see...	Jeg vil gjerne se ... yai vil *yarr*-neh say

48

Questions

What is that?	Hva er det?
	vah arr *day*?
How old is it?	Hvor gammelt er det?
	voorr *gah*-mehlt arr day?
Can I take photographs?	Kan jeg ta bilder?
	kahn yai tah *bil*-dehrr?
What time does it open/ close?	Når åpner/stenger den?
	norr *ohp*-nehrr/*stehng*-ehrr dehn?

Going Out

What's there to do in the evenings?	Hva kan man gjøre om kvelden?
	vah kahn mahn *yer*-rreh ohm kvehl-n?
How much does it cost to get in?	Hvor mye koster det for å komme inn?
	voor *mü*-eh *kos*-tehrr day forr oh *ko*-meh *in*?

PHRASE BUILDER

I feel like going to ...	Jeg har lyst til å gå på ...	yai hahrr *lüst* til oh goh poh ...
a bar	bar	bahrr
a cafe	cafe	kah-*fay*
the cinema	kino	*chee*-noo
a (rock) concert	(rocke) konsert	(*rroh*-keh) kon-*sart*
a nightclub	nattklubb	*naht*-kloob
the opera	opera	oo-peh-*rrah*
the theatre	teater	tay-*ah*-törr
a restaurant	restaurant	reh-stow-rahng

Are there places where you can hear local music?	Er det noen steder der en kan høre på norsk musikk?
	arr day *noo*-ehn *stay*-dehrr darr ehn kahn *her*-rreh poh noshk *moo*-seek?
Let's go!	La oss sette i gang!
	lah oss *seh*-teh ee gahng!

Interests

What do you do in your spare time?	Hva gjør du i fritiden?
	vah *yer*-rr du ee *frree*-tee-dehn?
What sport do you play?	Hva slag idrett driver du med?
	vah shlahgs *ee*-drreht *drree*-vehrr du may?
basketball	basketball
	bah-skeht-*bahl*
boxing	boksing
	buk-sing
fishing	fisking
	fi-sking
hiking	turgåing
	toorr-goh-ing
reading	lesing
	lay-sing
sport	sport/idrett
	spoorrt/*ee*-drreht
the theatre	teater
	ti-*uh*-tehrr
writing	skriver
	skrri-vehrr

50

Shopping

Fast Phrases

How much is it ...?	Hvor mye koster det ...? *vorr* mü-eh *ko*-stehrr day ...?
I'd like to buy ...	Jeg vil gjerne ha ... yai vil *yarr*-neh hah ...
I'm just looking.	Jeg bare ser. yai bah-rreh *sayrr*.

In the Shop

Do you have others?	Har du andre? hahrr du *ahn*-drreh?
Can I look at it?	Kan jeg få se på det? kahn yai foh *say* poh day?
I don't like it.	Det liker jeg ikke. day *lee*-kehrr yai i-keh.
Can you write down the price?	Kan du skrive ned prisen? kahn du *skrree*-veh nay *prree*-sehn?
Do you accept credit cards?	Tar du kredittkort? *tahrr* du krreh-*dit*-kort?
Could you lower the price?	Kunne du sette ned prisen? *koo*-neh du *seh*-teh nay *prree*-sehn?
I don't have much money.	Jeg har ikke mye penger. yai *hahrr* i-keh mü-eh *pehng*-ehrr.

🔊 LISTEN FOR

Can I help you?	Kan jeg hjelpe deg? kahn yai *yehl*-peh dai?
Will that be all?	Var det noe annet? vahrr day noo-eh *ahnt*?
Would you like it wrapped?	Skal jeg pakke det inn for deg? skahl yai *pah*-keh day in forr dai?
Sorry, this is the only one.	Beklager, dette er den eneste. beh-*klah*-gehrr deh-teh arr dehn *ay*-neh-steh.
How much/many do you want?	Hvor mye/mange vil du ha? voor *mü*-eh/*mahng*-eh vil du *hah*?

It's broken.	Det er ødelagt. day arr *er*-deh-lahgt.
I'd like to return this, please.	Jeg vil gjerne bytte dette. yai vil *yarr*-neh *bü*-teh *deh*-teh.

Shops

bookshop	bokhandel *book*-hahn-dl
camera shop	fotoforretning *foo*-too-for-*rreht*-ning
clothing store	klesbutikk *klays*-boo-*teek*
delicatessen	delikatesse deh-li-kah-teh-seh
general store; shop	dagligvare *dah*-glee-vah-rreh

green grocer	grønnsakshandler
	grrern-sahks-*hahnd*-lehrr
laundry	renseri
	rrehn-sö-*rree*
market	marked
	mahrr-kehd
newsagency/	kiosk
stationers	chosk
pharmacy	apotek
	ah-poh-*tayk*
shoeshop	skotøyforretning
	skoo-töü-for-*rreht*-ning
supermarket	supermarked
	soo-pehrr-mahrr-kayd

Essential Groceries

batteries	batteri
	bah-teh-*rree*
bread	brød
	brrer
butter	smør
	smer-rr

Local Knowledge

Where to Shop

Where would you go for bargains?	Hvor har de gode tilbud?
	voorr hahrr dee *goo*-eh til-bood?
Where would you go for (souvenirs)?	Hvor får man kjøpt (suvenirer)?
	voorr for-rr mahn cherpt (soo-veh-*nee*-rrehrr)?

53

cheese	ost oost
chocolate	sjokolade shoo-koo-*lah*-deh
cooking oil	olje *ool*-yeh
flour (plain)	mel mayl
ham	skinke *sking*-keh
honey	honning *ho*-ning
jam	syltetøy *sül*-teh-tuü
matches	fyrstikker *fürr*-shti-kehrr
milk	melk mehlk
pepper	pepper *peh*-pehrr
rice	ris rrees
salt	salt sahlt
sugar	sukker *su*-kehrr

Clothing

clothing	klær klarr
coat	frakk frrahk

dress	kjole *choo*-leh
jacket	jakke *yah*-keh
jumper (sweater, jersey)	genser *gehn*-sörr
shirt	skjorte *shorr*-teh
shoes	sko skoo
skirt	skjørt sher-rrt
trousers	bukser *buk*-sörr

Souvenirs

earrings	øredobber err-rreh-do-behrr
glasswork	glasstøy glahs-tuü
handicraft	kunsthåndverk koonst-hohnd-vark
necklace	halskjede hahls-chay-deh
Norwegian vest	kofte kof-teh
pottery	steintøy stain-tuü
ring	ring rring
rug	rye *rrü*-eh

Materials

cotton	bomull *boh*-mull
handmade	håndlaget *hohn-lah*-geht
leather	lær larr
brass	messing *meh*-sing
gold	gull gul
silver	sølv serlv
silk	silke sil-keh
wool	ull ul

Colours

black	svart svahrt
blue	blå bloh
brown	brun brroon
green	grønn grrern
pink	rosa *rroo*-sah
red	rød rrer

white	hvit
	veet
yellow	gul
	gool

Toiletries

comb	kam
	kahm
condoms	kondom
	kohn-dohm
deodorant	deodorant
	day-oo-doh-rrahnt
hairbrush	hårbørste
	hor-rr-bersh-teh
razor	barberhøvel
	bahrr-bayrr-her-vehl
sanitary napkins	damebind
	dah-mö-bin
shampoo	sjampo
	shahm-poo
shaving cream	barberkrem
	bahrr-bayrr-krraim
soap	såpe
	soh-peh
sunblock cream	solkrem
	sool-krraim
tampons	tamponger
	tahm-pong-ehrr
tissues	papirlommetørkle
	pah-peerr-lu-meh-ter-rr-kleh
toilet paper	dopapir
	doo-pah-peerr

toothbrush	tannbørste
	tahn-bersh-teh
toothpaste	tannkrem
	tahn-krraim

Stationery & Publications

map	kart
	kahrt
newspaper	avis
	ah-*vees*
newspaper in English	engelskspråklig avis
	ehng-ehlsk-sprroh-klee ah-*vees*
novels in English	engelske romaner
	ehng-ehl-ske rroh-*mah*-nehrr
paper	papir
	pah-*peerr*
pen (ballpoint)	penn (kulepenn)
	pehn (*koo*-leh-pehn)
scissors	saks
	sahks

Sizes & Comparisons

My size is (40).	Jeg bruker størrelse (førti).
	yai *broo*-kehrr *ster-rr*-ehl-seh (*fer-rr*-tee).
small	liten
	lee-tn
medium	medium
	may-dee-oom
large	stor
	stoorr

It doesn't fit. Det passer ikke.
day *pah*-sehrr i-keh.

PHRASE BUILDER

It's too ...	Det er for ...	day arr forr ...
big	stort	stoort
small	lite	*lee*-teh
short	kort	kort
long	langt	lahngt
tight	tettsittende	*teht*-si-tehn-eh
loose	løst	lerst

---

heavy	tung tung	
light	lett leht	
more	mer mayrr	
less	mindre *min*-dreh	
too much/many	for mye/mange forr *mü*-eh/*mahng*-eh	
many	mange *mahng*-ö	
enough	nok nok	
also	også *oh*-soh	
a little bit	litt lit	

Practicalities

⇒ Fast Phrases

Is there wi-fi access here?	Er det wi-fi tilgang her? *arr day wai-fai til-gahng harr?*
Where's the nearest ATM?	Hvor er nærmeste bankautomat? *voorr arr narr-meh-steh bahnk-ow-too-maht?*
Where are the toilets?	Hvor er toalettene/wc? *voor arr too-ah-leh-teh-neh/ vay-say?*

Banking

I want to exchange some money/travellers cheques.	Jeg vil gjerne veksle penger/heve noen reisesjekker. *yai vil yarr-neh vehk-sleh pehng-ehrr/hay-veh noo-ehn rrai-seh-sheh-kehrr.*
What is the exchange rate?	Hva er valutakursen? *vah arr vah-loo-tah-koorr-shehn?*
How many Norwegian kroner per dollar?	Hvor mange kroner for en dollar? *voorr mahng-eh krroo-nehrr forr ehn do-lahrr?*

Telephone

I want to ring ...	Jeg vil ringe til ... yai vil *rring*-eh til ...
The number is ...	Nummeret er ... *nu*-meh-rreh arr ...
How much does a three-minute call cost?	Hvor mye koster en tre minutters samtale? voorr *mü*-eh *ko*-stehrr ehn tray mi-*noo*-tehrrs *sahm*-tah-leh?
How much does each extra minute cost?	Hvor mye koster hvert ekstra minutt? voor *mü*-eh *ko*-stehrr vart *ehk*-strah mi-*noot*?
I'd like to speak to (Mr Olsen).	Jeg skulle gjerne få snakke med (herr Olsen). yai *sku*-leh *yarr*-neh foh *snah*-keh may (harr *ool*-sehn).
I want to make a reverse-charges phone call.	Jeg vil bestille en samtale med noteringsoverføring. yai vil beh-*sti*-leh ehn *sahm*-tah-leh may noo-*tay*-rrings-oo-vehrr-*fer*-rring.
It's engaged.	Det er opptatt. day arr *up*-taht.
I've been cut off.	Samtalen ble brutt. *sahm*-tah-lehn blay *brrut*.

Internet

Where can I get Internet access?	Hvor kan jeg få adgang til Internet? voorr kahn yai foh *ahd*-gahng til *in*-tehrr-neht?

| I'd like to send an email. | Jeg vil gjerne sende en email.
yai vil *yarr*-neh *sehn*-deh ehn ee-mayl. |

Post

I'd like some stamps.	Jeg vil gjerne ha noen frimerker. yai vil *yarr*-neh *hah* noo-ehn *frree*-mehrr-kehrr.
How much does it cost to send this to ...?	Hvor mye koster det å sende dette til ...? voorr *mü*-eh ko-stehrr day oh *sehn*-neh deh-teh til ...?
air mail	luftpost *luft*-post
envelope	konvolutt kon-vo-*loot*
mail box	postkasse *post*-kah-seh

PHRASE BUILDER

I'd like to send a ...	Jeg skal sende ...	yai skahl *sehn*-eh ...
letter	et brev	eht *brrayv*
parcel	en pakke	ehn *pah*-keh
postcard	et postkort	eht *post*-kort

Emergencies

Help!	Hjelp! *yehlp!*
Go away!/Buzz off!	Forsvinn!/Stikk av! *foh-shvin!/stik-ahv!*
Thief!	Tyv! *tüv!*
There's been an accident!	Det har skjedd en ulykke! *day hahrr shehd ehn oo-lü-keh!*
Call a doctor!	Ring en lege! *rring ehn lay-geh!*
Call an ambulance!	Ring etter en sykebil! *rring eh-tehrr ehn sü-keh-beel!*
I've been raped.	Jeg har blitt voldtatt. *yai hahrr blit vol-taht.*
I've been robbed.	Jeg harr blitt ranet. *yai hahrr blit rah-neht.*
Call the police!	Ring politiet! *rring poo-li-tee-eh!*
Where is the police station?	Hvor er politistasjonen? *voorr arr poo-li-tee-stah-shoon-ehn?*
I'm/My friend is sick.	Jeg er/Vennen min er syk. *yai arr/veh-nehn meen arr sük.*
Where are the toilets?	Hvor er toalettene/wc? *voore arr too-uh-leh-teh-neh/vay-say?*
Could you help me please?	Kan du hjelpe meg? *kahn du yehl-peh mai?*
I'm lost.	Jeg har gått meg vill. *yai hahrr got mai vil.*
Could I please use the telephone?	Kan jeg få låne telefonen? *kahn yai foh loh-neh teh-leh-foo-nehn?*

63

I'm sorry.	Jeg er lei for det. yay arr *lai* forr day.
I didn't realise I was doing anything wrong.	Jeg var ikke klar over at jeg gjorde noe galt. yai vahrr i-keh *klahrr* oh-vehrr aht yai *yoo*-rreh noo-eh *gahlt.*
I didn't do it.	Jeg har ikke gjort det. yai hahrr i-keh *yoorrt* day.
I wish to contact my embassy/consulate.	Jeg vil kontakte ambassaden min/ konsulatet mitt. yai vil kon-*tahk*-teh ahm-bah-*sah*-dehn meen/ koon-su-*lah*-teh mit.
I speak English.	Jeg snakker engelsk. yai snah-kehrr *ehng*-ehlsk.
My ... was stolen.	... er stjålet. ... arr *styor*-leht.
I have medical insurance.	Jeg har sykeforsikring. yai hahrr *sü*-keh-forr-*si*-krring.

PHRASE BUILDER

I've lost my ...   Jeg har mistet ...   yai hahrr *mis*-teht ...

bags	bagasjen min	bah-*gah*-shehn meen
handbag	vesken min	*veh*-skehn meen
money	pengene mine	*pehng*-eh-neh *mee*-neh
travellers cheques	reise-sjekkene mine	*rrai*-seh-sheh-keh-neh *mee*-neh
passport	passet mitt	*pah*-seh mit

My possessions are insured.	Eiendelene mine er forsikret. *ai*-ehn-*day*-leh-neh *mee*-neh arr forr-*shi*-krreht.
Where is the ...?	Hvor er ...? voor arr ...?
chemist	apoteket ah-poo-*tay*-keh
dentist	tannlegen *tahn*-lay-gehn
doctor	legen *lay*-gehn
hospital	sykehuset *sü*-keh-*hoo*-seh

Paperwork

address	adresse ah-*drreh*-seh
age	alder *ahl*-dehrr
birth certificate	fødselsattest *fert*-sehls-ah-*tehst*
border	grense *grrehn*-seh
car owner's title	vognkort *vogn*-kort
car registration	kjennetegn *cheh*-neh-tayn
customs	toll *tol*
date of birth	fødselsdato *fert*-sehls-dah-too

driver's licence	førerkort *fer*-rrehrr-kort
identification	legitimasjon lay-gi-ti-ma-*shoon*
immigration	innvandring *in*-vahn-drring
marital status	sivilstand si-*veel*-stahn
name	navn nahvn
nationality	nasjonalitet nah-shoo-nah-li-*tayt*
passport (number)	pass(nummer) *pahs*(-nu-mehrr)
place of birth	fødested *fer*-deh-stayd
profession	yrke *ürr*-keh
reason for travel	hensikt med reisen *hehn*-sikt may *rrai*-sehn
religion	religion rreh-li-*gyoon*
sex	kjønn chern
tourist card	turistkort too-*rrist*-kort
visa	visum *vee*-sum

Abbreviations

AS	**company**
EF	**EC**
e.Kr./f.Kr.	**AD/BC**
FN	**UN**
f.o.m.	**from (eg. today)**
gt./vn.	**St/Rd**
Herr/Fru	**Mr/Mrs/MS**
m.o.h.	**metres above sea level**
NAF	**AA (Automobile Association)**
nord/sør	**Nth/Sth**
NSB	**Norwegian Railway Company**

Health

Could I see a female doctor?	Kan jeg få snakke med en kvinnelig lege? kahn yai foh *snah*-keh may ehn *kvi*-neh-lee *lay*-geh?
What's the matter?	Hva er i veien? vah arr ee *vai*-ehn?
Where does it hurt?	Hvor gjør det vondt? *voorr* yer-rr day *voont*?
It hurts here.	Dette gjør vondt. day yer-rr voont *harr*.
My ... hurts.	Det gjør vondt i ... day yer-rr *voont* ee ...

PHRASE BUILDER

I have ...	Jeg har ...	yai hahr ...
an allergy	en allergi	ehn ah-lehrr-*gee*
anaemia	blodmangel	*bloo*-mahng-l
asthma	astma	*ahst*-mah
a burn	et brennsår	eht *brrehn*-sor-rr
a cold	snue	*snoo*-eh
constipation	forstoppelse	forr-*shto*-pehl-seh
a cough	hoste	*hoo*-steh
diabetes	sukkersyke/ diabetes	*su*-kehrr-*sü*-keh/ dee-ah-*bay*-tehs
diarrhoea	magesjau	*mah*-geh-show
epilepsy	fallesyke/ epilepsi	*fuh*-leh-sü-keh/ eh-peh-lehp-*see*
a fever	feber	*fay*-behrr
a headache	vondt i hodet	*voont* ee *hoo*-deh
hepatitis	gulsott	*gool*-soot
indigestion	dårlig fordøyelse	*dorr*-lee forr-*döy*-ehl-seh
an infection	en betennelse	ehn beh-*tehn*-ehl-seh
influenza	influensa	in-floo-*ehn*-sah
low/high blood pressure	lavt/høyt blodtrykk	*lahft*/*höyt* *bloo*-trrük
a pain	smerte	*smarr*-teh
a sore throat	vondt i halsen	*voont* ee *hahl*-sehn
a sprain	en forstuing	ehn forr-*stoo*-ing
sunburn	solbrenthet	*sool*-brrehnt-hayt
worms	innvollsmark	*in*-vols-mahrrk

Parts of the Body

ankle	ankelen *ahng*-keh-lehn
arm	armen *ahrr*-mehn
back	ryggen *rrüg*-gehn
chest	brystkassa *brrüst*-kah-sah
ear	øret *er*-rreh
eye	øyet *öy*-eh
finger	fingeren *fing*-eh-rrehn
foot	foten *foo*-tn
hand	hånda *hoh*-nah
head	hodet *hoo*-deh
heart	hjertet *yarr*-teh
leg	beinet *bai*-neh
mouth	munnen *mu*-nehn
nose	nesa *nay*-suh
teeth	tennene *teh*-neh-neh
throat	halsen *hahl*-sehn

Useful Phrases

I'm allergic to (antibiotics/penicillin).	Jeg er allergisk mot (antibiotika/penicillin). yai arr ah-*lehrr*-gisk moot (ahn-tee-bee-*oo*-ti-kah/*peh*-ni-si-*leen*).
I'm pregnant.	Jeg er gravid. yai arr grrah-*veed*.
I'm on the pill.	Jeg tar P-pillen. yai tahrr *pay*-pi-lehn.
I have been vaccinated.	Jeg er vaksinert. yai arr vahk-si-*nayrt*.
I feel better.	Jeg føler meg bedre. yai *fer*-lehrr mai *bay*-drreh.
I feel worse.	Jeg føler meg verre. yai *fer*-lehrr mai *varr*-eh.

At the Chemist

I need medication for ...	Jeg trenger medisin for ... yai *trrehng*-ehrr meh-di-seen forr ...
I have a prescription.	Jeg har en resept. yai hahrr ehn rreh-*sehpt*.
accident	ulykke *oo*-lü-keh
addiction	avhengighet ahv-*hehng*-ee-hayt
aspirin	dispril dis-*prril*
bandage	bandasje bahn-*dah*-sheh

blood test	blodprøve *bloo*-prrer-vö
contraceptive	prevensjonsmiddel prray-vehn-*shoons*-midl
injection	sprøyte *sprröy*-tö
menstruation	menstruasjon/mens mehns-trroo-uh-*shoon*/mens

At the Dentist

I have a toothache.	Jeg har tannpine. yai hahrr *tahn*-pee-neh.
I've lost a filling.	Jeg har mistet en fylling. yai hahrr mi-steht ehn *fü*-ling.
I've broken a tooth.	Jeg har ødelagt en tann. yai hahrr *er*-deh-lahgt ehn tahn.

Dictionary

ENGLISH to NORWEGIAN

- a -

accommodation overnatting *oh-vörr-nah-ting*
account konto *kohn-too*
aeroplane fly *flü*
afternoon ettermiddag *eht-törr-mi-dahg*
air-conditioned klimaanlegg *klee-mah-ahn-lehg*
airport flyplass *flü-plahss*
airport tax flyplassavgift *flü-plahss-ahv-yift*
alarm clock vekkerklokke *veh-kehrr-klo-keh*
alcohol alkohol *ahl-koo-hool*
antique antikk *ahn-teek*
appointment avtale *ahv-tah-leh*
arrivals ankomst *ahn-kohmst*

art gallery kunstgalleri *kunst-gah-lö-rree*
ashtray askebeger *ahs-keh-bay-görr*
at på poh
ATM minibank mi-nee-*bangk*
autumn høst herst

- b -

baby baby *bai-bee*
back (body) rygg rrüg
backpack ryggsekk *rrüg-sehk*
bad dårlig *dohrr-lee*
bag pose *poh-seh*
baggage bagasje bah-*gah*-sheh
baggage allowance tillatt bagasje *ti-laht-bah-gah*-sheh
baggage claim bagasjeutlevering bah-*gah*-sheh-oot-leh-vehrr-ing
bakery bakeri bah-keh-*rree*
Band-Aid plaster *plah*-störr
bank bank bahngk

ank account bankkonto
ahng-kohn-too
ath badekar *bah-deh-kahrr*
athroom bad bahd
attery batteri bah-teh-*rree*
each strand strrahn
eautiful vakker/vakkert
ah-kehrr/vah-kehrt
eauty salon skjønnhetssalong
hun-hayt-sah-long
ed seng sehng
ed linen sengetøy sehng-eh-*tuū*
edroom soverom *soh-veh-rroom*
eer øl erl
icycle sykkel *sü-kehl*
ig stor stoorr
ill regning *rrai-ning*
irthday bursdag/fødselsdag
örsh-dahg/ferd-sehls-dahg
lack svart svahrt
lanket teppe *teh-peh*
lood group blodtype *bloo-tü-peh*
lue blå bloh
oarding house gjestgiveri
ehst-yee-veh-rree
oarding pass
mbordstigningskort
hm-boorr-steeg-nings-koort
oat båt boht
ook bok book
ook (make a booking) bestille
eh-sti-leh
ooked up fullt fult
ookshop bokhandel *book-hahndl*
order grense *grrehn-*seh
ottle flaske *flah-skeh*
ox eske *eh-skeh*
oy gutt gut
oyfriend kjæreste *cha-rreh-steh*
ra bh bay-hoh
rakes bremser *brrehm-*sörr
read brød brrer

briefcase stresskoffert
strehs-koo-fört
broken ødelagt *er-deh-lahgt*
brother bror brroorr
brown brun brroon
building bygning *büg-*ning
bus (city) bybuss *bü-*buss
bus (intercity) buss bus
bus station busstasjon
*bu-*sta-shoon
bus stop bussholdeplass
bus-hoh-leh-plahs
business bedrift beh-*drift*
business class businessklasse
bis-nes-klah-seh
busy opptatt/travel
opp-taht/trah-vehl
butcher's shop slakter *slahk-*törr

- C -

cafe cafe *kah-fay*
call ringe *ring-*eh
camera kamera *kah-mö-rrah*
can (tin) boks boks
can opener boksåpner *boks-*orp-
nehrr
cancel avlyse *ahv-lü-seh*
car bil beel
car hire bilutleie *beel-oot-lai-eh*
car owner's title vognkort
*vongn-*kort
car registration kjennetegn
*chehn-*neh-tayn
cash kontant kohn-*tahnt*
cashier kasserer *kah-seh-*rrehr
chairlift (skiing) skiheis *shee-*hais
change skifte/bytte
shif-teh/bü-teh
change (coins) veksel *vehk-*sehl
change (money) veksel *vehk-*sehl

73

check sjekke *sheh-keh*
check (banking) sjekk *shehk*
check-in (desk) innsjekk *in-shehk*
cheque sjekk *shehk*
child barn *bahrrn*
church kirke *chirr-kö*
cigarettes sigaretter
si-gah-rreht-törr
cigarette lighter sigarettenner
si-gah-rreht-teh-nörr
cigarette papers rullepapir *rrul-lö-puh-pee-rr*
city by *bü*
city centre sentrum *sehn-trum*
clean rein *rrain*
cleaning rydding/rensing
rer-ding/rehn-sing
cloakroom garderobe
gahrr-deh-rroo-beh
closed stengt *stehngt*
clothing klær *klarr*
coat frakk *frrahk*
coffee kaffe *kah-feh*
coins mynter *mün-törr*
cold kald/kaldt *kahl/kahlt*
comfortable behagelig/
komfortabel *beh-hah-geh-lee/
kohm-fohr-tah-behl*
company selskap *sehl-skahp*
computer datamaskin/PC
dah-tah-mah-sheen/pay-say
condom kondom *kohn-dohm*
confirm (a booking) bekrefte
beh-krrehf-teh
connection forbindelse
fohr-bin-dehl-seh
convenience store kiosk *chosk*
cook (chef) kokk *kohk*
cook (make food) lage mat
lah-geh-maht
cool kjølig *chu-lee*
cough hoste *hohs-teh*

countryside landsbygd
lahns-bügd
cover charge inngangspenger
in-gahngs-pehng-ehr
crampons brodder *brruh-dör*
crafts håndverk *hohnd-vehrk*
credit card kredittkort
krreh-dit-kort
currency exchange valutaveksling
vah-loo-tah-vehk-sling
customs toll *tol*

-d-

daily daglig *dah-glee*
date dato *dah-too*
date of birth fødselsdato
fert-söls-dah-too
daughter datter *daht-tehr*
day dag *dahg*
day after tomorrow (the)
overimorgen *oh-vehr-ee-mohrn*
day before yesterday forgårs
fohr-gohrsh
delay forsinkelse *fohr-sink-ehl-seh*
delicatessen delikatesse-
deh-li-kuh-tehs-seh
depart dra/reise *drah/rai-seh*
department store kjøpesenter
chö-peh-sehn-tehrr
departure avgang *ahv-gahng*
deposit innskudd *in-gahng*
diaper bleie *blai-eh*
dictionary ordbok *oorr-book*
dining car spisevogn
spee-sö-vongn
dinner middag *mid-dahg*
direct direkte *di-rrehk-tö*
dirty skitten *shit-n*
discount rabatt *rah-baht*
dish rett *reht*

octor lege lay-geh
og hund hün
ouble bed dobbeltseng
ob-bölt-sehng
ouble room dobbeltrom
ob-bölt-rohm
ress kjole choo-lö
rink drikke dri-keh
rink (beverage) drikk drik
rivers licence førerkort
örr-ehrr-kort
runk full fül
ry tørr ter-rr

-e-

ach hver vehrr
arly tidlig tee-lee
ast øst öst
at spise spee-seh
conomy class økonomiklasse
e-koh-noh-mee-klah-seh
levator heis hais
mbassy ambassade
hm-bah-sah-dö
ngineer ingeniør in-shö-nyörr
nglish engelsk ehng-ehlsk
nough nok nok
ntry inngang in-gahng
nvelope konvolutt kon-vu-lut
evening kveld kvehl
very hver vehrr
everything alt ahlt
xcess (baggage) ekstrabagasje
hk-strah-bah-gah-sheh
xchange veksling vehk-sling
exhibition utstilling oot-stil-ing
xit utgang oot-gahng
xpensive dyr dürr
xpress (mail) A-post ah-pohst

-f-

fall falle fah-leh
family familie fuh-mee-li-eh
fare billett bi-leht
fashion mote moh-teh
fast fort fort
father far fahrr
ferry ferje fehrr-yö
fever feber fay-behrr
film (for camera) film film
fine (penalty) bot boot
finger finger fing-ör
firewood ved vay
first class første klasse
fersh-teh-klah-seh
fish shop fiskehandler
fi-skeh-hahnd-lehrr
flashlight) lommelykt lum-mö-lükt
fleamarket loppemarked
lo-peh-mahr-kehd
flight flight flait
floor (storey) etasje eh-tah-sheh
flu influensa in-floo-ehn-sah
footpath gangsti gahng-stee
foreign utenlandsk
oo-tehn-lahnsk
forest skog skoog
free (at liberty) fri free
free (gratis) gratis grah-tis
fresh fersk fehrshk
friend venninne/venn
vehn-nin-nö/vehn

-g-

garden hage hah-geh
gas bensin behn-seen
gas (for cooking) gass gahs
gas cartridge propanbeholder
prroo-pahn-beh-hoh-lehrr

75

gift gave *gah*-veh
girl jente *yehn*-teh
girlfriend kjæreste *cha*-rreh-steh
glasses (spectacles) briller
brri-lehrr
gloves hansker *hahn*-skehrr
go gå goh
go out gå ut goh oot
go shopping handle *hahn*-dleh
gold gull gul
grateful takknemlig
tahk-*nehm*-lee
gray grå groh
green grønn grrern
grocery dagligvare
dah-glee-vah-rreh
guesthouse gjestehus
ye-stö-hoos
guided tour omvisning
ohm-vees-ning

-h-

half halv hahl
handsome kjekk chehk
heated oppvarmet
ohp-vahrr-meht
help hjelp yehlp
here her haerr
highway motorvei *moo*-toor-vai
hire leie *lai*-eh
holidays ferie/helligdager
fay-rree-eh/*heh*-lee-dah-görr
honeymoon hvetebrødsdager
vay-teh-brrers-dah-görr
hospital sykehus *sü*-keh-hoos
hot varmt vahrmt
hotel hotell hoh-*tehl*
hour time *tee*-meh
husband mann muhn

-i-

ice axe isøks *ees*-erks
identification legitimasjon
lay-gi-ti-*muh*-shoon
identification card (ID) ID-kort
ee-day-kort
ill syk sük
included inkludert in-kloo-*daert*
information informasjon
in-foor-mah-*shoon*
insurance forsikring fohrr-*si*-kring
intermission pause *pow*-seh
Internet cafe internettkafe
in-tehr-neht-kah-*fay*
interpreter tolk tohlk
itinerary reiserute
rai-seh-roo-teh

-j-

jacket jakke *yah*-keh
jeans jeans/dongeribukser
jeens/*dong*-eh-rreh-bük-sörr
jewellery smykker *smü*-körr
journey reise *rai*-seh
jumper genser *gehn*-sörr

-k-

key nøkkel *ner*-köl
kind snill snil
kitchen kjøkken *chö*-kehn

-l-

lane felt fehlt
large stor stoorr
last (previous) forrige
foh-rree-eh

late sein sain
later seinere *sai*-neh-rreh
launderette vaskeri
vah-skeh-*rree*
laundry (clothes) klesvask
klays-vahsk
leather lær larr
leave reise *rai*-seh
left luggage (office) gjenglemt
bagasje *yehn*-glehmt bah-*gah*-sheh
letter brev brrayv
lighter lighter lai-*törr*
lift heis hais
linen (material) lin leen
locked låst lohst
look for se etter say *eh*-tehrr
lost mistet *mist*-eht
lost property office hittegods
hi-teh-goods
luggage bagasje bah-*gah*-sheh
luggage lockers bagasjeskap
bah-*gah*-sheh-skahp
lunch lunsj lernsh

- m -

mail (postal system) post pohst
make-up sminke *smink*-eh
man mann muhn
manager (restaurant, hotel)
daglig leder *dah*-glee *lay*-dehrr
map (of country) kart kahrt
map (of town) bykart *bü*-kahrt
market torget *törr*-geh
meal måltid *mohl*-tee
meat kjøtt chert
medicine (medication) medisin
meh-di-*seen*
metro station T-banestasjon
tay-bah-neh-stah-*shoon*
midday klokka tolv klok-*kah* tol

midnight midnatt *mid*-naht
milk melk mehlk
mineral water mineralvann
mi-neh-*rrahl*-vahn
mobile phone mobiltelefon
moo-*beel*-teh-leh-foon
modem modem *moh*-dehm
money penger *pehng*-ehrr
month måned *moh*-nehd
morning morgen morn
mother mor moorr
motorcycle motorsykkel
moh-toor-sü-kehl
motorway motorvei *moh*-toor-vai
mountain fjell fyehl
museum museum moo-*say*-oom
music shop musikkbutikk
moo-*sik*-boo-tik

- n -

name navn nahvn
napkin serviett sehrr-vee-*eht*
nappy bleie *blai*-eh
newsagent aviskiosk
ah-*vees*-chosk
newspaper avis ah-*vees*
next (month) neste *neh*-steh
nice snill snil
night natt naht
night out (on the town) ute på
byen *oo*-teh poh *bü*-ehn
nightclub nattklubb *naht*-kloob
no vacancy fullt fült
non-smoking ikke røyking
i-keh *röü*-king
noon klokka tolv klok-kuh *tol*
north nord noorr
now nå noh
number tall/nummer
tahl/*noo*-mehrr

- o -

office kontor kohn-*tor*
oil olje *ul*-yeh
one-way ticket enveisbillett
ayn-vais-bi-leht
open åpen oh-pehn
opening hours åpningstider
ohp-nings-tee-dehrr
orange (colour) oransje
oo-*rahn*-sheh
out of order i ustand ee oo-stahn

- p -

painter maler *mah*-lehrr
painting (a work) male *mah*-leh
painting (the art) maleri
mah-leh-*rree*
pants bukser bük-sörr
pantyhose strømpebukser
strerm-peh-bük-sörr
paper papir pah-*peerr*
party fest fehst
passenger passasjer pah-sah-*shayrr*
passport pass pahs
passport number passnummer
pahs-noo-mehrr
path sti stee
penknife lommekniv *lum*-mö-kneev
pensioner pensjonist
pehn-shoh-*nist*
performance forestilling
fohr-eh-sti-ling
petrol bensin behn-*seen*
petrol station bensinstasjon
behn-*seen*-stah-shoon
phone book telefonkatalog
teh-leh-*foon*-kah-tah-lohg
phone box telefonkiosk
teh-leh-*foon*-chosk

phone card telefonkort
teh-leh-*foon*-kort
phone charger telefonlader
teh-leh-*foon*-lah-dehrr
phrasebook lommeparlør
luh-meh-pahrr-lerl
picnic piknik *pik*-nik
pillow pute poo-teh
pillowcase putetrekk
poo-teh-trehk
pink rosa *rroo*-sah
platform plattform *plaht*-form
play (theatre) skuespill
skoo-eh-spil
police officer (in city)
politibetjent poo-li-*tee*-beh-tyehnt
police officer (in country)
lensmann *lehns*-mahn
police station politistasjon
poo-li-*tee*-stah-shoon
post code postnummer
pohst-noo-mehrr
post office postkontor
pohst-kohn-*tor*
postcard postkort *pohst*-kort
pound (money, weight) pund
poond
prescription resept reh-*sehpt*
present gave *gah*-veh
price pris prees

- q -

quick rask rahsk

- r -

receipt kvittering kvi-*tehrr*-ing
red rød rrer
refund refusjon rreh-foo-*shoon*
rent leie *lai*-eh

repair reparere *rreh-pah-rray-rreh*
retired pensjonert *pehn-shoo-naert*
return returnere *rreh-toorr-nay-rreh*
return (ticket) retur *rreh-toorr*
road vei *vai*
robbery tyveri *tü-veh-rree*
room rom *rroom*
room number romnummer *rroom-noo-mehrr*
rope tow tau
route rute *rroo-teh*

~ S ~

safe trygg *trög*
Scotland Skottland *skoht-lahn*
sea sjø *sher*
season sesong/årstid *seh-song/ohrsh-tee*
seat (place) sete *say-teh*
seatbelt setebelte *say-teh-behl-teh*
self service selvbetjening *sehl-beh-tyeh-ning*
service service *sirr-vis*
service charge serviceavgift *sirr-vis-ahv-yift*
share dele *day-leh*
shirt skjorte *shohr-teh*
shoe sko skoo
shop butikk *boo-teek*
shopping centre kjøpesenter *cher-peh-seh-tehrr*
short (height) kort kort
show show shoh
shower dusj doosh
sick syk *sük*
silk silke *sil-keh*

silver sølv *serl*
single (person) singel *sing-ehl*
single room enkeltrom *ehn-kehlt-rroom*
sister søster *sers-tehrr*
size (general) størrelse *stö-rrehl-seh*
skirt skjørt *shört*
sleeping bag sovepose *soo-veh-poo-seh*
sleeping car sovevogn *soo-veh-vohgn*
slide (film) lysbilde *lüs-bil-deh*
smoke røyke *röü-keh*
snack mellommåltid *meh-lohm-mohl-tee*
snow snø sner
socks sokker *so-kehrr*
son sønn sern
soon snart snahrt
south sør ser-rr
spring (season) vår vohrr
square (town) torg tohrrg
stairway trappegang *trrah-peh-gahng*
stamp frimerke *free-mehrr-keh*
stationer's (shop) kontorrekvisita *kohn-tor-rreh-kvi-si-tah*
stolen stjålet *styoh-leht*
stove kokeplater *koo-keh-plah-tehrr*
stranger fremmed *freh-mehd*
street gate *gah-teh*
student student *stoo-dehnt*
subtitles undertekster *oon-örr-tehk-stehr*
suitcase koffert *koh-fört*
summer sommer *sohm-mehrr*
supermarket supermarked *soo-pehrr-mahrr-kayd*
surface mail (land) B-post *bay-pohst*

surface mail (sea) B-post
bay-pohst
surname etternavn *eh-tehrr-nahvn*
sweater genser *gehn-sörr*
swim svømme *sver-meh*
swimming pool svømmebaseng
sver-meh-bah-seng

- t -

tall høy herü
taxi stand taxiholdeplass
tahk-see-hoh-leh-plahss
teacher lærer *la-rrörr*
teller funksjonær *foonk-shoo-narr*
tent telt tehlt
tent pegs teltplugger *tehlt-plu-gehrr*
ticket billett bi-*leht*
ticket machine billettautomat
bi-*leht*-ow-toh-*maht*
ticket office billettkontor
bi-*leht*-kohn-*torr*
time tid tee
timetable tidsplan *tids*-plahn
tip (gratuity) tips/driks tips/driks
to til til
today i dag i-*dahg*
together sammen *sah*-mehn
tomorrow i morgen i-*morn*
torch lommelykt *lum*-mö-lükt
tour omvisning *ohm*-vees-ning
tourist office turistkontor
too-rist-kohn-torr
towel håndkle *hohn*-klay
town by bü
train station togstasjon
tohg-stah-*shoon*
transit lounge transitsalong
trahn-*sit*-sah-*long*
travel agency reisebyrå
rai-seh-bü-*roh*

travellers cheque reisesjekk
rai-seh-shehk
trip tur toorr
trousers bukser *book*-sörr
twin beds to enkeltsenger
toh-*ehng*-kehlt-seng-ehrr

- u -

underwear undertøy *oo*-narr-tuü

- v -

vacant ledig *lay*-dee
vacation ferie *fay*-ree-eh
vacation (holidays) ferie
fay-ree-eh
validate godkjenne *goo*-kyeh-neh
vegetable grønnsak *grern*-sahk
view utsikt *oot*-sikt

- w -

waiting room venterom
vehn-teh-rroom
walk gå goh
warm varm vahrrm
wash (something) vaske *va*-skeh
washing machine vaskemaskin
va-skeh-mah-*sheen*
watch klokke *klo*-keh
water vann vahn
water bottle vannflaske *vahn*-flah-skeh
way vei vai
week uke oo-keh
west vest vehst
what hva vah
when når nohrr
where hvor voorr

which hvilken/hvilket/hvilke *vil-kehn/vil-keht/vil-keh*
white hvit *veet*
who hvem *vehm*
why hvorfor *voor-for*
wife kone *koo-nö*
wifi wifi *wai-fai*
window vindu *vin-doo*
wine vin *veen*
winter vinter *vin-törr*
without uten *oo-tehn*

woman kvinne *kvi-neh*
wool ull *ool*
wrong (direction) feil *fail*

- y -

year år *ohrr*
yesterday i går *i-gor-rr*
youth hostel vandrerhjem *vahn*-drehrr-yehm*

Dictionary

NORWEGIAN *to* ENGLISH

-*a*-

alkohol ahl-koo-*hool* alcohol
alt ahlt everything
ambassade ahm-bah-sah-dö embassy
ankomst *ahn*-kohmst arrivals
antikk ahn-*teek* antique
åpen *oh*-pehn open
åpningstider *ohp*-nings-tee-dehrr opening hours
A-post *ah*-pohst express (mail)
år ohrr year
årstid *ohrsh*-tee season
askebeger *ahs*-keh-bay-görr ashtray
avgang *ahv*-gahng departure
avis ah-*vees* newspaper
aviskiosk ah-*vees*-chosk newsagent
avlyse *ahv*-lü-seh cancel
avtale *ahv*-tah-leh appointment

-*b*-

baby *bai*-bee baby
bad bahd bathroom
badekar *bah*-deh-kahrr bath
bagasje bah-*gah*-sheh baggage
bagasje bah-*gah*-sheh luggage
bagasjeskap bah-*gah*-sheh-skahp luggage lockers
bagasjeutlevering bah-*gah*-sheh-oot-leh-vehrr-ing baggage claim
bakeri bah-keh-*rree* bakery
bank bahngk bank
bankkonto *bahng*-kohn-too bank account
barn bahrrn child
båt boht boat
batteri bah-teh-*rree* battery
bedrift beh-*drift* business
behagelig beh-*hah*-geh-lee comfortable
bekrefte beh-*krrehf*-teh confirm (a booking)

ensin behn-*seen* gas
ensin behn-*seen* petrol
ensinstasjon behn-*seen*-stah-
hoon petrol station
estille beh-*sti*-leh
ook (make a booking)
h bay-hoh bra
il beel car
illett bi-*leht* fare
illett bi-*leht* ticket
illettautomat bi-*leht*-ow-toh-
naht ticket machine
illettkontor bi-*leht*-kohn-*torr*
cket office
ilutleie *beel*-oot-*lai*-eh car hire
lå bloh blue
leie *blai*-eh diaper
leie *blai*-eh nappy
lodtype *bloo*-tü-peh
lood group
ok book book
okhandel *book*-hahndl
ookshop
oks boks can (tin)
oksåpner *boks*-orp-nehrr can
pener
ot boot fine (penalty)
-post *bay*-pohst
urface mail (land)
-post *bay*-pohst
urface mail (sea)
remser brrehm-sörr brakes
rev brrayv letter
riller brri-lehrr
glasses (spectacles)
rød brrer bread
rodder brruh-dör crampons
ror brroorr brother
run brroon brown
ukser bük-sörr pants
ukser *book*-sörr trousers
ursdag börsh-dahg birthday

businessklasse bis-nes-klah-*seh*
business class
buss bus bus (intercity)
bussholdeplass bus-hoh-leh-*plahs*
bus stop
busstasjon bu-sta-shoon
bus station
butikk boo-*teek* shop
by bü city
by bü town
bybuss bü-buss bus (city)
bygning *büg*-ning building
bykart *bü*-kahrt map (of town)
bytte *bü*-teh change

- d -

dag dahg day
daglig *dah*-glee daily
daglig leder *dah*-glee *lay*-dehrr
manager (restaurant, hotel)
dagligvare *dah*-glee-vah-rreh
grocery
dårlig *dohrr*-lee bad
datamaskin dah-tah-mah-*sheen*
computer
dato *dah*-too date
datter *daht*-tehr daughter
dele *day*-leh share
delikatesse- deh-li-kuh-*tehs*-seh
delicatessen
direkte di-*rrehk*-tö direct
dobbeltrom dob-bölt-rohm
double room
dobbeltseng dob-bölt-sehng
double bed
dongeribukser *dong*-eh-rree-bük-
sörr jeans
dra drah depart
drikk drik drink (beverage)
drikke *dri*-keh drink
driks driks tip (gratuity)

dusj doosh shower
dyr dürr expensive

- e -

ekstrabagasje ehk-strah-bah-gah-sheh excess (baggage)
engelsk ehng-ehlsk English
enkeltrom ehn-kehlt-rroom single room
enveisbillett ayn-vais-bi-leht one-way ticket
eske eh-skeh box
etasje eh-tah-sheh floor (storey)
ettermiddag eht-törr-mi-dahg afternoon
etternavn eh-tehrr-nahvn surname

- f -

falle fah-leh fall
familie fuh-mee-li-eh family
far fahrr father
feber fay-behrr fever
feil fail wrong (direction)
felt fehlt lane
ferie fay-ree-eh vacation
ferie fay-ree-eh vacation (holidays)
ferie fay-rree-eh holidays
ferje fehrr-yö ferry
fersk fehrshk fresh
fest fehst party
film film film (for camera)
finger fing-ör finger
fiskehandler fi-skeh-hahnd-lehrr fish shop
fjell fyehl mountain
flaske flah-skeh bottle
flight flait flight
fly flü aeroplane

flyplass flü-plahss airport
flyplassavgift flü-plahss-ahv-yift airport tax
fødselsdag ferd-sehls-dahg birthday
fødselsdato fert-söls-dah-too date of birth
forbindelse fohr-bin-dehl-seh connection
førerkort förr-ehrr-kort drivers licence
forestilling fohr-eh-sti-ling performance
forgårs fohr-gohrsh day before yesterday
forrige foh-rree-eh last (previous)
forsikring fohrr-si-kring insurance
forsinkelse fohr-sink-ehl-seh delay
første klasse fersh-teh-klah-seh first class
fort fort fast
frakk frrahk coat
fremmed freh-mehd stranger
fri free free (at liberty)
frimerke free-mehrr-keh stamp
full fül drunk
fullt fult booked up
fullt fült no vacancy
funksjonær foonk-shoo-narr teller

- g -

gå goh go
gå goh walk
gå ut goh oot go out
gangsti gahng-stee footpath
garderobe gahrr-deh-rroo-beh cloakroom
gass gahs gas (for cooking)

gate *gah*-teh street
gave *gah*-veh gift
gave *gah*-veh present
genser *gehn*-sörr jumper
genser *gehn*-sörr sweater
gjenglemt bagasje *yehn*-glehmt bah-*gah*-sheh left luggage (office)
gjestehus *ye*-stö-hoos guesthouse
gjestgiveri *yehst*-yee-veh-*rree* boarding house
godkjenne *goo*-kyeh-neh validate
grå groh gray
gratis *grah*-tis free (gratis)
grense *grrehn*-seh border
grønn *grrern* green
grønnsak *grern*-sahk vegetable
gull gul gold
gutt gut boy

- h -

hage *hah*-geh garden
halv hahl half
håndkle *hohn*-klay towel
handle *hahn*-dleh go shopping
håndverk *hohnd*-vehrk crafts
hansker *hahn*-skehrr gloves
heis hais elevator
heis hais lift
helligdager *heh*-lee-dah-görr holidays
her haerr here
hittegods *hi*-teh-goods lost property office
hjelp yehlp help
høst herst autumn
hoste *hohs*-teh cough
hotell hoh-*tehl* hotel
høy herü tall
hund hün dog

hva vah what
hvem vehm who
hver vehrr each
hver vehrr every
hvetebrødsdager *vay*-teh-brrers-dah-görr honeymoon
hvilken/hvilket/hvilke *vil*-kehn/*vil*-keht/*vil*-keh which
hvit veet white
hvor voorr where
hvorfor *voor*-for why

- i -

i dag i-*dahg* today
i går i-*gor*-rr yesterday
i morgen i-*morn* tomorrow
i ustand ee oo-stahn out of order
ID-kort ee-day-kort identification card (ID)
ikke røyking *i*-keh *röü*-king non-smoking
influensa in-floo-*ehn*-sah flu
informasjon in-foor-mah-*shoon* information
ingeniør *in*-shö-nyörr engineer
inkludert in-kloo-*daert* included
inngang *in*-gahng entry
inngangspenger *in*-gahngs-pehng-ehr cover charge
innsjekk *in*-shehk check-in (desk)
innskudd *in*-gahng deposit
internettkafe in-tehr-neht-kah-*fay* Internet cafe
isøks *ees*-erks ice axe

- j -

jakke *yah*-keh jacket
jeans jeens jeans
jente *yehn*-teh girl

-k-

kaffe *kah*-feh coffee
kald/kaldt kahl/kahlt cold
kamera *kah*-mö-rrah camera
kart kahrt map (of country)
kasserer kah-*seh*-rrehr cashier
kiosk chosk convenience store
kirke *chirr*-kö church
kjæreste *cha*-rreh-steh boyfriend
kjæreste *cha*-rreh-steh girlfriend
kjekk chehk handsome
kjennetegn *chehn*-neh-tayn
car registration
kjøkken *chö*-kehn kitchen
kjole *choo*-lö dress
kjølig *chu*-lee cool
kjøpesenter *chö*-peh-sehn-tehrr
department store
kjøpesenter *cher*-peh-seh-tehrr
shopping centre
kjøtt chert meat
klær klarr clothing
klesvask *klays*-vahsk
laundry (clothes)
klimaanlegg *klee*-mah-ahn-*lehg*
air-conditioned
klokka tolv klok-*kah* tol midday
klokka tolv klok-kuh *tol* noon
klokke *klo*-keh watch
koffert *koh*-fört suitcase
kokeplater koo-keh-*plah*-tehrr
stove
kokk kohk cook (chef)
komfortabel *kohm*-fohr-tah-behl
comfortable
kondom kohn-*dohm* condom
kone *koo*-nö wife
kontant kohn-*tahnt* cash
konto *kohn*-too account
kontor kohn-*tor* office

kontorrekvisita kohn-*tor*-rreh-kvi-si-tah stationer's (shop)
konvolutt kon-vu-*lut* envelope
kort kort short (height)
kredittkort krreh-*dit*-kort
credit card
kunstgalleri *kunst*-gah-lö-*rree*
art gallery
kveld kvehl evening
kvinne kvi-neh woman
kvittering kvi-*tehrr*-ing receipt

-l-

lær larr leather
lærer *la*-rrörr teacher
lage mat *lah*-geh-maht
cook (make food)
landsbygd *lahns*-bügd
countryside
låst lohst locked
ledig *lay*-dee vacancy
ledig *lay*-dee vacant
lege lay-geh doctor
legitimasjon lay-gi-ti-*muh*-shoon
identification
leie *lai*-eh hire
leie *lai*-eh rent
lensmann *lehns*-mahn
police officer (in country)
lin leen linen (material)
lommekniv *lum*-mö-kneev
penknife
lommelykt *lum*-mö-lükt torch
(flashlight)
lommeparlør *luh*-meh-pahrr-lerl
phrasebook
loppemarked *lo*-peh-mahr-kehd
fleamarket
lunsj lernsh lunch
lysbilde *lüs*-bil-deh slide (film)

- m -

male *mah*-leh painting (a work)
maler *mah*-lehrr painter
maleri mah-leh-*rree*
painting (the art)
måltid *mohl*-tee meal
måned *moh*-nehd month
mann muhn husband
mann muhn man
medisin meh-di-*seen*
medicine (medication)
melk mehlk milk
mellommåltid *meh*-lohm-mohl-tee
snack
middag *mid*-dahg dinner
midnatt *mid*-naht midnight
mineralvann mi-neh-*rrahl*-vahn
mineral water
minibank mi-nee-*bangk* ATM
mistet *mist*-eht lost
mobiltelefon moo-*beel*-teh-leh-
foon mobile phone
modem *moh*-dehm modem
mor moorr mother
morgen morrn morning
mote *moh*-teh fashion
motorsykkel *moh*-toor-sü-kehl
motorcycle
motorvei *moo*-toor-vai highway
motorvei *moh*-toor-vai motorway
museum moo-*say*-oom museum
musikkbutikk moo-*sik*-boo-tik
music shop
mynter *mün*-törr coins

- n -

nå noh now
når nohrr when

natt naht night
nattklubb *naht*-kloob nightclub
navn nahvn name
neste *neh*-steh next (month)
nok nok enough
nøkkel *ner*-köl key
nord noorr north

- o -

ødelagt *er*-deh-lahgt broken
økonomiklasse ö-koh-noh-*mee*-
klah-seh economy class
øl erl beer
nummer *noo*-mehrr number
olje *ul*-yeh oil
ombordstigningskort ohm-*boorr*-
steeg-nings-koort boarding pass
omvisning *ohm*-vees-ning
guided tour
omvisning *ohm*-vees-ning tour
opptatt *opp*-taht busy
oppvarmet *ohp*-vahrr-meht heated
oransje oo-*rahn*-sheh
orange (colour)
ordbok *oorr*-book dictionary
øst öst east
overimorgen *oh*-vehr-ee-mohrn
day after tomorrow (the)
overnatting *oh*-vörr-nah-ting
accommodation

- p -

på poh at
papir pah-*peerr* paper
pass pahs passport
passasjer pah-sah-*shayrr*
passenger

passnummer *pahs*-noo-mehrr passport number

pause *pow*-seh intermission

PC pay-say computer

penger *pehng*-ehrr money

pensjonert pehn-shoo-*naert* retired

pensjonist pehn-shoh-*nist* pensioner

piknik *pik*-nik picnic

plaster *plah*-störr Band-Aid

plattform *plaht*-form platform

politibetjent poo-li-*tee*-beh-tyehnt police officer (in city)

politistasjon poo-li-*tee*-stah-shoon police station

pose *poh*-seh bag

post pohst mail (postal system)

postkontor pohst-kohn-*tor* post office

postkort *pohst*-kort postcard

postnummer *pohst*-noo-mehrr post code

pris prees price

propanbeholder prroo-*pahn*-beh-hoh-lehrr gas cartridge

pund poond pound (money, weight)

pute *poo*-teh pillow

putetrekk *poo*-teh-trehk pillowcase

- *r* -

rabatt rah-*baht* discount

rask rahsk quick

refusjon rreh-foo-*shoon* refund

regning *rrai*-ning bill

rein rrain clean

reise *rai*-seh journey

reise *rai*-seh leave, depart

reisebyrå *rai*-seh-bü-*roh* travel agency

reiserute *rai*-seh-roo-teh itinerary

reisesjekk *rai*-seh-shehk travellers cheque

rensing *rehn*-sing cleaning

reparere rreh-pah-*rray*-rreh repair

resept reh-*sehpt* prescription

rett reht dish

retur rreh-*toorr* return (ticket)

returnere rreh-toorr-*nay*-rreh return

ringe *ring*-eh call

rød rrer red

rom rroom room

romnummer *rroom*-noo-mehrr room number

rosa *rroo*-sah pink

røyke *röü*-keh smoke

rute *rroo*-teh route

rydding *rer*-ding cleaning

rygg rrüg back (body)

ryggsekk *rrüg*-sehk backpack

- *s* -

sammen *sah*-mehn together

se etter say eh-tehrr look for

sein sain late

seinere *sai*-neh-rreh later

selskap *sehl*-skahp company

selvbetjening *sehl*-beh-tyeh-ning self service

seng sehng bed

sengetøy sehng-eh-*tuü* bed linen

sentrum *sehn*-trum city centre

service *sirr*-vis service

serviceavgift *sirr*-vis-ahv-yift service charge

serviett sehrr-vee-*eht* napkin

sesong seh-*song* season

sete say-teh seat (place)

setebelte say-teh-behl-teh seatbelt

show shoh show

sigarettenner si-gah-*rreht*-teh-nörr cigarette lighter

silke sil-keh silk

singel sing-ehl single (person)

sjekk shehk check (banking)

sjekk shehk cheque

sjekke sheh-keh check

sjø sher sea

skifte shif-teh change

skiheis shee-hais chairlift (skiing)

skitten shit-n dirty

skjønnhetssalong shun-*hayt*-sah-*long* beauty salon

skjørt shört skirt

skjorte shohr-teh shirt

sko skoo shoe

skog skoog forest

Skottland skoht-lahn Scotland

skuespill skoo-eh-spil play (theatre)

slakter slahk-törr butcher's shop

sminke smink-eh make-up

smykker smü-körr jewellery

snart snahrt soon

snill snil kind

snill snil nice

snø sner snow

sokker so-kehrr socks

sølv serl silver

sommer sohm-mehrr summer

sønn sern son

sør ser-rr south

søster sers-tehrr sister

sovepose soo-veh-poo-seh sleeping bag

soverom soh-veh-rroom bedroom

sovevogn soo-veh-vohgn sleeping car

spise spee-seh eat

spisevogn spee-sö-vongn dining car

stengt stehngt closed

sti stee path

stjålet styoh-leht stolen

stor stoorr big

stor stoorr large

størrelse stö-rrehl-seh size (general)

strand strrahn beach

stresskoffert strehs-koo-fört briefcase

strømpebukser strerm-peh-bük-sörr pantyhose

student stoo-*dehnt* student

supermarked soo-pehrr-mahrr-kayd supermarket

svart svahrt black

svømme sver-meh swim

svømmebaseng sver-meh-bah-seng swimming pool

syk sük ill

syk sük sick

sykehus sü-keh-hoos hospital

sykkel sü-kehl bicycle

takknemlig tahk-*nehm*-lee grateful

- t -

tall tahl number

taxiholdeplass tahk-see-hoh-leh-plahss taxi stand

tau tow rope

T-banestasjon tay-bah-neh-stah-*shoon* metro station

89

telefonkatalog teh-leh-*foon*-kah-tah-lohg phone book
telefonkiosk teh-leh-*foon*-chosk phone box
telefonkort teh-leh-*foon*-kort phone card
telefonlader teh-leh-*foon*-lah-dehrr phone charger
telt tehlt tent
teltplugger tehlt-*plu*-gehrr tent pegs
teppe *teh*-peh blanket
tid tee time
tidlig *tee*-lee early
tidsplan tids-plahn timetable
til til to
tillatt bagasje ti-laht-bah-*gah*-sheh baggage allowance
time *tee*-meh hour
tips tips tip (gratuity)
to enkeltsenger toh-*ehng*-kehlt-seng-ehrr twin beds
togstasjon tohg-stah-*shoon* train station
tolk tohlk interpreter
toll tol customs
torg tohrrg square (town)
torget *törr*-geh market
tørr ter-rr dry
transitsalong trahn-*sit*-sah-*long* transit lounge
trappegang *trrah*-peh-gahng stairway
travel *trah*-vehl busy
trygg tsrög safe
tur toorr trip
turistkontor too-rist-kohn-torr tourist office
tyveri *tü*-veh-rree robbery

- u -

uke *oo*-keh week
ull ool wool
undertekster *oon*-örr-tehk-stehr subtitles
undertøy *oo*-narr-tuü underwear
ute på byen oo-teh poh *bü*-ehn night out (on the town)
uten *oo*-tehn without
utenlandsk *oo*-tehn-lahnsk foreign
utgang *oot*-gahng exit
utsikt *oot*-sikt view
utstilling *oot*-stil-ing exhibition

- v -

vakker/vakkert *vah*-kehrr/*vah*-kehrt beautiful
valutaveksling vah-*loo*-tah-vehk-sling currency exchange
vandrerhjem *vahn*-drehrr-yehm youth hostel
vann vahn water
vannflaske *vahn*-flah-skeh water bottle
vår vohrr spring (season)
varm vahrrm warm
varmt vahrmt hot
vaske *va*-skeh wash (something)
vaskemaskin *va*-skeh-mah-*sheen* washing machine
vaskeri vah-skeh-*rree* launderette
ved vay firewood
vei vai road, way
vekkerklokke *veh*-kehrr-klo-*keh* alarm clock
veksel *vehk*-sehl change (coins)

veksel *vehk*-sehl change (money)
veksling *vehk*-sling exchange
venninne/venn vehn-*nin*-nö/vehn
friend
venterom *vehn*-teh-rroom
waiting room
vest vehst west
vin veen wine

vindu *vin*-doo window
vinter *vin*-törr winter
vognkort *vongn*-kort
car owner's title

-*w*-

wifi wai-fai wifi

Acknowledgments
Associate Product Director Angela Tinson
Product Editor Kate Chapman
Language Writers Daniel Cash, Sarah Corbisier,
Runa Eilertsen, Doekes Lulofs
Cover Designer Campbell McKenzie
Cover Researcher Gwen Cotter

Thanks
Gwen Cotter, James Hardy, Sandie Kestell, Kate Kiely, Indra Kilfoyle,
Anne Mason, Wibowo Rusli, Saralinda Turner, Juan Winata

Published by Lonely Planet Global Ltd
CRN 554153

2nd Edition – April 2024
Text © Lonely Planet 2024
Cover Image Senja, Troms og Finnmark; Roberto Moiola/
Sysaworld/Getty Images ©

Printed in China   10 9 8 7 6 5 4 3 2 1

Contact lonelyplanet.com/contact

MIX
Paper from
responsible sources
FSC™ C021741

Index

10. Phrases to Get You Talking

Hello.	Goddag. *goo-dahg.*
Goodbye.	Ha det. *hah-day.*
Please.	Vær så snill. *varr shoo snil.*
Thank you.	Takk. *tahk.*
Excuse me.	Unnskyld. *un-shül.*
Sorry.	Beklager. *beh-klah-gehrr.*
Yes.	Ja. *yah.*
No.	Nei. *nai.*
I don't understand.	Jeg forstår ikke. *yai for-stohrr i-keh.*
How much is it?	Hvor mye koster det? *vorr mü-eh ko-stehrr day?*